# ARTIFICIAL INTELLIGENCE BASICS

## A Step-by-Step Introduction to AI for Beginners

## THOMPSON CARTER

# TABLE OF CONTENTS

# INTRODUCTION

**Artificial Intelligence Basics: A Step-by-Step Introduction to AI for Beginners"**

## 1. The Rise of Artificial Intelligence: An Overview

In the last few decades, the world has experienced a monumental shift driven by technological advancements. Among the most revolutionary technologies shaping our future, **Artificial Intelligence (AI)** stands out as one of the most disruptive and transformative. Once relegated to the realms of science fiction, AI has become an integral part of our everyday lives, influencing the way we work, communicate, learn, and make decisions. Whether we are interacting with voice assistants like **Siri** or **Alexa**, receiving personalized content recommendations on **Netflix**, or experiencing self-driving cars, AI is woven into the fabric of modern existence.

Artificial Intelligence is not a single technology but a collection of methods and algorithms that allow machines to perform tasks typically requiring human intelligence. These tasks include reasoning, problem-solving, perception, learning, and natural language understanding. Over the past few years, AI has gone from being an academic pursuit to a central player in industries such as healthcare, entertainment, finance, and logistics, among many others. Its vast applications are only beginning to be explored, and the implications of its capabilities are profound, promising both immense opportunities and significant challenges.

This book is designed to introduce the concepts of AI in a way that makes it accessible to beginners. AI is often viewed as a complex and intimidating field, with advanced mathematics and programming at its core. However, AI is becoming increasingly user-friendly, and its foundational concepts can be grasped without a technical background. This book will demystify AI, break down the foundational knowledge, and guide you step-by-step through the key concepts and tools you need to understand and engage with the field of Artificial Intelligence.

## 2. Understanding the Growing Importance of AI

AI's rapid adoption in industries worldwide speaks to its potential to drive innovation, create efficiencies, and solve complex problems. From **automating repetitive tasks** to **enhancing decision-making**, AI is providing new solutions that were once thought impossible. Its ability to analyze and process large volumes of data far exceeds human capabilities, enabling businesses and governments to gain insights, predict trends, and make informed decisions faster than ever before.

The influence of AI is particularly apparent in the following domains:

- **Healthcare**: AI is aiding doctors in diagnosing diseases, predicting patient outcomes, and discovering new drugs. With AI-powered tools, medical professionals can identify patterns in medical data that may otherwise go unnoticed, potentially saving lives and improving treatment efficiency.

- **Finance**: In the financial sector, AI is used to predict market trends, manage portfolios, detect fraud, and automate customer service. AI-driven algorithms provide personalized recommendations, making financial services more accessible and efficient.

- **Transportation**: The rise of **autonomous vehicles** is perhaps one of the most visible applications of AI. AI systems are powering self-driving cars, drones, and intelligent traffic management systems, promising to reshape the future of mobility.

- **Entertainment**: From content recommendations to AI-generated music and movies, AI is transforming the entertainment industry. Platforms like **Netflix**, **Spotify**, and **YouTube** use AI to personalize content for users, making entertainment more engaging.

- **Smart Devices**: The proliferation of **Internet of Things (IoT)** devices, such as smart thermostats, wearables, and home assistants, relies heavily on AI. These devices learn from user behavior and adapt to improve the user experience, making homes more efficient and connected.

While these applications illustrate AI's power, the journey to AI's widespread use is far from over. **Ethical considerations**, such as **privacy** concerns, **job displacement**, and **bias in AI systems**, also present challenges that must be addressed as AI continues to evolve.

---

### 3. The Structure and Purpose of the Book

This book aims to provide a clear, accessible, and practical introduction to the field of Artificial Intelligence for beginners. The purpose is not to overwhelm the reader with overly technical jargon, but to build a strong foundation of knowledge that will serve as a springboard for further exploration. Whether you are a student, a professional looking to expand your skillset, or simply someone interested in learning about the transformative power of AI, this book will guide you through the essentials and beyond.

The book is structured to introduce core concepts, tools, and techniques in a logical progression. We will begin with an **overview of AI**—its history, evolution, and core ideas—before diving into specific subfields such as **machine learning (ML), deep learning, natural language processing (NLP)**, and **computer vision**. Throughout the chapters, we will provide hands-on examples, real-world applications, and exercises to reinforce the concepts discussed.

Each chapter will break down complex ideas into digestible sections, making use of:

- **Step-by-step guides** for hands-on learning.
- **Practical examples** that showcase AI in real-world scenarios.
- **Exercises and challenges** that test understanding and foster deeper engagement with the material.

Additionally, we will highlight **tools** and **resources** for learning AI, focusing on free and accessible platforms, such as **Google Colab**, **Kaggle**, and **TensorFlow**, where readers can experiment and build their own AI models.

The chapters have been carefully crafted to build on one another, progressing from foundational knowledge to more advanced topics. By the end of this book, readers will not only understand AI concepts but also feel confident in using AI tools to solve real-world problems.

---

## 4. AI Fundamentals: Laying the Groundwork

Before diving into AI's technicalities, we'll start by covering the **fundamental concepts** that every aspiring AI enthusiast must understand:

- **What is AI?**: Defining AI and understanding its distinction from other computational fields, such as robotics and automation.

- **Types of AI**: Exploring the different categories of AI, from **narrow AI (weak AI)**, which focuses on specific tasks, to **general AI (strong AI)**, which aims for human-level cognitive abilities.

- **History and Evolution of AI**: Tracing the development of AI, from early concepts in the 1950s to modern breakthroughs in machine learning and deep learning.

These introductory sections will provide readers with a solid grasp of the AI landscape, setting the stage for deeper dives into specialized areas.

---

### *5. AI in Action: Practical Applications Across Industries*

As we progress, we will explore how AI is actively shaping various industries and domains. Through real-world examples and case studies, we will illustrate how AI is used to solve critical problems and revolutionize industries:

- **Healthcare**: Discussing AI's role in diagnostics, personalized medicine, and drug discovery. We'll explore how tools like **IBM Watson** are helping healthcare professionals make informed decisions and how AI-powered medical devices are improving patient outcomes.

- **Finance**: Exploring AI applications in **fraud detection**, **algorithmic trading**, and **customer service**. AI's ability to predict trends and analyze financial data is transforming the financial landscape, and we'll see how companies use AI to gain a competitive edge.

- **Education**: AI in education is personalizing learning experiences for students. From **adaptive learning platforms** to **AI-powered tutors**, we will examine how these innovations are shaping the future of education.

- **Transportation**: The development of **self-driving vehicles** and **autonomous drones** is one of the most exciting AI applications. This section will cover the current state of autonomous transportation and its future potential.

- **Entertainment**: AI is revolutionizing how media is created and consumed. We will discuss AI-driven content recommendation engines and **AI in game development** and **film production**.

Through these industry-specific discussions, readers will gain a clear understanding of how AI is solving complex problems and creating new possibilities in the world.

# CHAPTER 1: INTRODUCTION TO ARTIFICIAL INTELLIGENCE

### *What is AI?*

Artificial Intelligence (AI) refers to the simulation of human intelligence in machines that are programmed to think and learn. In essence, AI is the capability of a machine to imitate intelligent human behavior. At its core, AI involves creating algorithms that allow computers to perform tasks that typically require human intelligence, such as understanding natural language, recognizing images, making decisions, and solving complex problems.

AI can be classified into different types based on its capabilities:

- **Narrow AI**: Also known as weak AI, this type of AI is designed to handle specific tasks. Most AI systems today, like Siri or recommendation engines, are examples of narrow AI.
- **General AI**: This is the kind of AI seen in science fiction, capable of performing any intellectual task that a human can. General AI is still a theoretical concept and doesn't exist yet.

- **Superintelligent AI**: A hypothetical AI that surpasses human intelligence across all fields. This concept is still largely speculative.

### *Historical Overview of AI*

The journey of AI has been long and filled with both breakthroughs and setbacks. Here's a brief timeline of key moments in AI's development:

1. **1950s: The Beginnings**
   - **Alan Turing**: Often regarded as the father of AI, Turing proposed the **Turing Test** in 1950 as a way to measure a machine's ability to exhibit intelligent behavior indistinguishable from a human.
   - **John McCarthy**: Coined the term "Artificial Intelligence" in 1956 and organized the **Dartmouth Conference**, which is considered the birth of AI as an academic field.

2. **1960s - 1970s: Early Optimism**
   - Researchers like **Marvin Minsky** and **Allen Newell** developed early AI systems that could solve basic problems or play games like chess. These systems, however, lacked the sophistication we expect today.
   - The **"AI Winter"**: A period in the 1970s and 1980s when enthusiasm around AI cooled due to the lack

of progress and the inability to meet early high expectations.

3. **1990s - 2000s: Resurgence and Specialization**

   o AI began to find practical applications in specific fields. Notable examples include **IBM's Deep Blue**, which defeated the world chess champion Garry Kasparov in 1997.

   o Machine learning algorithms also began to improve, thanks to advances in computing power and the availability of large datasets.

4. **2010s - Present: Deep Learning and the AI Boom**

   o **Deep learning** revolutionized AI. By using neural networks with many layers (hence "deep"), AI systems achieved breakthroughs in areas like image and speech recognition. Google's **AlphaGo** beat the world champion in the game of Go, a major milestone for AI.

   o The rise of **big data** and **cloud computing** provided the infrastructure needed for AI to flourish, and companies like **Google**, **Amazon**, and **Tesla** began using AI in everyday products.

*Real-World Examples: AI in Smartphones and Recommendation Systems*

AI is no longer a concept confined to labs or research institutions—it's integrated into our everyday lives. Here are two key examples of AI that many people encounter regularly:

1. **AI in Smartphones**:
   - **Voice Assistants**: Siri (Apple), Google Assistant, and Alexa use natural language processing (NLP) to understand spoken commands and provide responses. These systems rely on AI to interpret voice data, answer questions, and control other apps or devices.
   - **Camera Features**: Modern smartphones, like the iPhone or Google Pixel, use AI-powered image recognition and enhancement. For example, AI helps in **portrait mode** by blurring the background to highlight the subject, and AI algorithms can adjust lighting and focus for better pictures in various environments.

2. **Recommendation Systems**:
   - **Streaming Platforms**: Services like **Netflix**, **Spotify**, and **YouTube** use AI to recommend content based on your previous viewing or listening history. By analyzing data such as what you've watched or liked, these platforms create personalized recommendations that keep users engaged.

○ **E-Commerce**: AI powers recommendation engines in platforms like **Amazon** and **eBay**, suggesting products based on your browsing behavior and purchases. AI analyzes vast amounts of user data, including past behavior, to predict items that you might be interested in.

This chapter introduced Artificial Intelligence—defining what AI is, its evolution over the years, and its transformative role in society today. From voice assistants in our smartphones to recommendation systems shaping our online experiences, AI is not just a technological concept; it's part of the fabric of our daily lives. In the upcoming chapters, we will explore how AI works, the algorithms behind it, and the vast range of applications it has in modern society.

# CHAPTER 2: THE FOUNDATIONS OF AI: UNDERSTANDING MACHINES

*Key Concepts of AI*

To grasp how AI works, it's important to understand some foundational concepts that form the building blocks of AI systems. These concepts are fundamental to how machines process information, learn from data, and make decisions.

1. **Algorithm**: An algorithm is a step-by-step procedure or set of rules that a computer follows to solve a problem or complete a task. In AI, algorithms are used to process data, make predictions, or even make decisions. The efficiency and accuracy of these algorithms determine how well an AI system performs.

   o **Example**: A sorting algorithm in an AI system could be used to arrange data in a way that allows the system to better recognize patterns or trends in that data.

2. **Data**: AI thrives on data. It's the raw material that machines use to learn. The more data an AI system has, the more it can improve its performance over time. The process of feeding data into an AI system to help it "learn" is central to the field of machine learning.

   o **Real-World Example**: When using AI for a voice assistant, data such as voice recordings and commands are collected and processed to improve the assistant's ability to understand and respond accurately.

3. **Model**: In AI, a model is a mathematical representation of a process or system. Machine learning models are trained using large datasets, and over time, these models improve their ability to make predictions or decisions based on the data they have seen.

   o **Example**: A facial recognition model uses images of faces to learn what features to look for in order to accurately identify individuals.

4. **Learning**: Learning in AI refers to how machines improve over time based on the data they receive. There are different types of learning techniques, such as supervised, unsupervised, and reinforcement learning, each suited for different types of problems.

> o **Example**: A recommendation system on Netflix "learns" your viewing preferences and suggests movies you might enjoy based on past data.

5. **Intelligence**: In the context of AI, intelligence refers to the ability of a machine to perform tasks that would normally require human cognitive processes, like reasoning, learning, and decision-making. The goal is to create systems that mimic human-like thinking and problem-solving.

## *How Machines "Learn" and Make Decisions*

Machines, especially those built using AI, learn through a process of training on data, and their decision-making abilities are based on the patterns they uncover during that training. Here's a simple breakdown of how this process works:

1. **Data Collection**: First, an AI system requires data. This data can be anything from images, text, and numbers to more complex inputs like sensor readings. The quality and quantity of data directly influence how well the system can learn.

> o **Example**: To teach a machine how to recognize cats in photos, you need to collect a large dataset of images that are labeled with either "cat" or "not cat."

2. **Training**: During training, the AI system processes the data and identifies patterns. For example, a machine learning algorithm might identify certain features, such as shapes, colors, or textures, that are commonly found in pictures of cats. It uses these patterns to improve its ability to make predictions.

   o **Example**: A machine learning algorithm could be trained on thousands of images of cats and dogs, and over time it will learn to recognize specific features that distinguish cats from dogs, like facial structure or body shape.

3. **Making Predictions**: Once trained, the AI system can apply what it has learned to make predictions or decisions. In a supervised learning setup, the system can predict outcomes for new, unseen data. For example, after being trained on labeled images of cats and dogs, the model can predict whether a new image contains a cat or a dog.

   o **Example**: A recommendation system, after being trained on a user's previous viewing habits, can predict what new movies or shows they might enjoy.

4. **Feedback and Improvement**: Feedback is crucial to refining AI models. If an AI makes a mistake, it learns from that mistake and adjusts its model accordingly. In some cases, feedback is immediate (e.g., through user input), while in others, it is learned over time.

o **Example**: In a self-driving car, sensors provide constant feedback about the car's environment, allowing the system to adjust its decisions in real-time to avoid accidents or navigate to the correct destination.

5. **Decision Making**: Once trained, AI systems can apply learned patterns to make decisions. Decision-making in AI typically involves processing information, applying learned models, and choosing an action that best solves the problem at hand. This process can be deterministic (based on a fixed set of rules) or probabilistic (based on patterns in data).

o **Example**: A voice assistant like Siri or Alexa makes decisions about how to respond based on the input received from a user's voice command, processing that information using natural language processing (NLP) techniques.

---

### Real-World Example: Smart Assistants like Siri or Alexa

Smart assistants like **Siri**, **Alexa**, and **Google Assistant** are prime examples of AI systems that use learning and decision-making techniques to help users perform tasks or access information more efficiently. Here's a breakdown of how they work:

1. **Voice Recognition**: When you speak to an AI assistant, the first task is to recognize your voice input. The system uses **natural language processing (NLP)** to interpret what you said and convert it into a format the machine can understand.

   o **Example**: If you say, "What's the weather like today?", the AI assistant breaks down the sentence into its components to understand the intent (weather query) and the specific details (the date).

2. **Understanding the Command**: After recognizing the voice input, the assistant needs to figure out the meaning behind it. NLP algorithms analyze the words, context, and tone to understand what you're asking.

   o **Example**: If you say, "Set an alarm for 7 AM," the system understands the action (set an alarm) and the specific time (7 AM).

3. **Making a Decision**: Once the AI understands your command, it uses its internal models to decide on the best course of action. This decision-making process is based on pre-programmed logic and learned behavior from past interactions.

   o **Example**: If you ask for the weather forecast, the assistant might query an online weather service and provide you with an accurate response.

4. **Continuous Learning**: Over time, AI assistants learn more about your preferences. For instance, if you frequently ask for traffic updates at certain times of the day, the assistant may proactively provide you with updates during those times.

   o **Example**: Based on your past behavior, Alexa might offer to play your favorite playlist as you wake up or offer suggestions for nearby coffee shops when you're driving.

---

This chapter has introduced the foundational elements that power AI systems: algorithms, data, models, and the process of machine learning. We've also explored how machines "learn" by processing data, identifying patterns, and making decisions, with smart assistants like Siri and Alexa serving as tangible examples. These systems are just one example of AI's ability to understand, learn, and respond in ways that make our lives more convenient and efficient. In the following chapters, we'll dive deeper into specific AI techniques and how they're applied in real-world scenarios.

# CHAPTER 3: TYPES OF AI: NARROW VS. GENERAL AI

*Differences Between Narrow (Weak) AI and General (Strong) AI*
Artificial Intelligence can be classified into two broad categories based on its capabilities: **Narrow AI (Weak AI)** and **General AI (Strong AI)**. Understanding the distinction between these two types of AI helps clarify their current applications and potential future developments.

1. **Narrow AI (Weak AI)**: Narrow AI refers to AI systems that are designed and trained to perform a specific task or set of tasks. These systems are highly specialized and excel at what they're designed to do, but they cannot generalize or perform tasks outside of their programmed scope.

Narrow AI systems do not possess any understanding or consciousness—they simply follow algorithms to solve problems.

- o **Characteristics**:
  - Task-specific
  - Operates within a limited range of functions
  - No ability to learn beyond its programmed capabilities
  - No consciousness or self-awareness
- o **Example**: Google search is a perfect example of Narrow AI. It's designed to search and rank web pages based on relevance to a query. Google search uses AI algorithms to understand the keywords in your query and return relevant results, but it can't perform tasks unrelated to web search, like controlling a robot or understanding complex conversations.
- o **Another Example**: A **recommendation system** on Netflix or Amazon is another example of Narrow AI. It analyzes your past behavior—what movies you've watched or products you've purchased—to predict and suggest what you might like next. However, it can't perform tasks outside of its recommendation function.

2. **General AI (Strong AI)**: General AI, often referred to as **Strong AI**, refers to an advanced form of AI that can perform any intellectual task that a human being can do. Unlike Narrow AI, which is constrained to specific tasks, General AI has the capability to learn and adapt to a wide variety of tasks, think critically, reason, and understand context. It is able to generalize from one task to another, applying knowledge across different domains and situations.

   o **Characteristics**:
     - Human-like versatility
     - Capable of performing any intellectual task
     - Can learn, adapt, and generalize knowledge across diverse areas
     - Theoretical concepts of consciousness and reasoning
     - No existing examples in practical applications (still a theoretical goal)

   o **Example**: An **autonomous robot** that can perform a wide range of tasks—like cooking, cleaning, and assisting in healthcare—would be an example of General AI. Such a robot would not only learn how to perform one task but also adapt to a variety of environments and tasks. This kind of AI could autonomously solve problems, make decisions, and even come up with creative solutions to unforeseen challenges.

---

## Real-World Examples: Narrow AI vs. General AI

1. **Google Search (Narrow AI)**: Google Search is a highly advanced example of Narrow AI. It utilizes complex algorithms to index web pages and rank them based on relevance to a user's search query. Here's how it works:

   o **Task-Specific**: Google Search is specifically built to help you find information on the web. It's great at this job because it's designed to understand your search queries, process vast amounts of data, and provide relevant links to websites, news articles, videos, etc.

   o **No Generalization**: While Google Search is incredibly effective at answering search queries, it cannot generalize beyond this function. It won't, for instance, help you with tasks like controlling smart devices, diagnosing diseases, or performing physical tasks like assembling furniture.

   o **AI Algorithms Involved**: Google uses AI techniques such as **natural language processing (NLP)**, **machine learning**, and **deep learning** to understand the context behind your query. It analyzes keywords, user intent, location, and even personal preferences to provide personalized results.

- o **Example**: If you search for "best pizza in New York," Google will provide you with results based on local data, reviews, and relevance. However, if you asked Google to perform a complex task like conducting a scientific experiment, the AI would not be capable of doing so.

2. **Autonomous Robots (General AI)**: General AI, on the other hand, remains a future goal and has not been realized yet, though there are attempts to create machines that exhibit more advanced capabilities. An autonomous robot is often used as an example to illustrate what General AI might look like. Here's how it would differ from Narrow AI:

- o **Versatility**: Unlike Narrow AI systems, which excel at only one task, General AI systems can perform a wide range of activities. For example, a robot with General AI could adapt to multiple roles such as caregiving, cleaning, cooking, and more. It would learn new tasks autonomously and adapt to new environments.

- o **Learning and Problem-Solving**: An autonomous robot equipped with General AI could solve novel problems that it has never encountered before, something Narrow AI cannot do. For instance, if a robot encounters an object in a new environment, it could figure out how to move around it or manipulate it without specific programming for that object.

- o **Reasoning and Decision-Making**: General AI would have the ability to make decisions in complex, unpredictable environments. For example, an autonomous robot in a disaster relief scenario could make decisions about which buildings to search first, how to navigate obstacles, and when to request help.

- o **Example**: **Sophia the Robot** (developed by Hanson Robotics) is one of the closest examples of an advanced AI humanoid robot, but even she is more an example of **advanced Narrow AI** rather than true General AI. While Sophia can hold conversations, recognize faces, and process a wide range of inputs, she still lacks the depth of reasoning, learning, and adaptive capabilities of General AI.

In this chapter, we've explored the key distinction between **Narrow AI** and **General AI**. Narrow AI is designed for specific tasks, excelling within those boundaries, while General AI aims to replicate human-like cognitive abilities, allowing for a broader scope of tasks and decision-making. **Google Search** is a prime example of Narrow AI, excelling at web searches but limited to this function. In contrast, **autonomous robots** represent a vision of General AI, with the potential to learn and adapt to diverse tasks, although this level of AI is still theoretical.

As we move forward, we'll continue to see advancements in Narrow AI, with its applications expanding across different industries. General AI remains a long-term goal, and while there are exciting strides being made in AI research, it's clear that we're still some distance away from achieving true General AI.

# CHAPTER 4: HOW AI THINKS: ALGORITHMS AND PROBLEM SOLVING

*What is an Algorithm?*

An **algorithm** is essentially a step-by-step set of instructions or rules designed to solve a problem or complete a specific task. In the context of AI, algorithms are the core of how AI systems make decisions, process data, and perform tasks. Every time an AI system takes an action or makes a prediction, it's using an algorithm to decide how to proceed.

Algorithms are the backbone of AI because they allow machines to perform tasks ranging from simple calculations to complex decision-making processes. These instructions define how an AI system processes input data, learns from it, and arrives at a solution.

- **Example**: When you use a search engine like Google, the algorithm determines how to rank pages based on their relevance to your query, considering factors like keywords, page content, user behavior, and links.

In AI, algorithms can be divided into different types based on their functionality:

1. **Search Algorithms**: Used to find solutions to problems by exploring different possibilities.
2. **Sorting Algorithms**: Organize data in a specific order, which is important for tasks like searching or finding patterns in data.
3. **Optimization Algorithms**: Designed to find the best possible solution given certain constraints.
4. **Learning Algorithms**: Enable the AI system to improve performance based on data.

---

*Problem-Solving Methods Used in AI*

AI problem-solving methods are varied and can be broadly categorized into several approaches. These methods allow AI to break down complex tasks into smaller, more manageable components and systematically arrive at a solution.

1. **Search Algorithms**: Search algorithms are used in AI to explore different possibilities and find the best solution to a problem. These algorithms can search through large spaces of possible solutions and pick the one that best fits the criteria.

   o **Example**: In playing chess, a search algorithm like **Minimax** is used to evaluate possible moves and predict the best move by analyzing the game tree. Minimax looks ahead at all possible moves and their outcomes to make a decision about the most optimal move.

   o **Real-World Example**: In pathfinding, AI uses search algorithms like *A (A-star)** to find the shortest path from one point to another on a map, whether for a robot navigating through an environment or for a navigation system on your phone.

2. **Heuristic Methods**: Heuristics are problem-solving techniques that simplify the search for solutions by focusing on the most promising paths or solutions. While heuristics don't guarantee the optimal solution, they allow

AI to find good enough solutions quickly, especially when the problem space is vast.

- o **Example**: In chess, a heuristic might be evaluating the strength of a move based on a limited number of factors, like the control of the center of the board or the safety of the king. This speeds up the decision-making process rather than analyzing every possible move in detail.

- o **Real-World Example**: Heuristic algorithms are used in Google search to prioritize results based on relevance and quality, rather than simply searching all data points equally.

3. **Optimization Algorithms**: Optimization algorithms are designed to find the best solution given a set of constraints. These algorithms are key in machine learning, where the goal is to find the parameters that minimize error or maximize accuracy.

- o **Example**: The **Gradient Descent** algorithm is commonly used in machine learning to minimize the error of predictions. It works by adjusting the model's parameters (such as weights in a neural network) step by step to reduce the difference between predicted and actual outcomes.

- o **Real-World Example**: In logistics, AI might use optimization to determine the most efficient route for delivering packages, minimizing both time and fuel consumption.

4. **Rule-Based Systems**: Rule-based systems solve problems using predefined rules. These rules are applied to specific inputs to generate outputs. AI systems using this method are typically deterministic, meaning the same input will always produce the same output.

   o **Example**: A chatbot with a rule-based system might use a set of if-then rules to respond to customer inquiries. For instance, if a customer asks for store hours, the bot replies with the store's hours based on a predefined rule in its programming.

   o **Real-World Example**: Expert systems in healthcare often use rule-based algorithms to diagnose diseases based on input symptoms. For instance, if a patient reports certain symptoms, the system might apply a rule like, "If fever + cough = possible flu" to suggest a diagnosis.

5. **Machine Learning-Based Methods**: Machine learning allows AI to solve problems by learning from data. Rather than following predefined rules, AI systems using machine learning identify patterns in the data and use them to make predictions or decisions.

   o **Example**: In AI-driven stock trading, machine learning algorithms analyze historical data on stock prices and trading volume, and then use this information to predict future price movements. The algorithm continually adjusts based on new data.

- o **Real-World Example**: Image recognition in AI uses machine learning to identify objects in photos or video. For example, self-driving cars use machine learning algorithms to recognize pedestrians, other vehicles, and road signs in real time.

---

*Example: AI Solving Puzzles or Games (e.g., Chess)*

One of the most well-known areas where AI demonstrates its problem-solving abilities is in games like **chess**. AI's ability to evaluate millions of possible moves and find the optimal strategy showcases its computational power.

1. **Chess as a Problem-Solving Task**: Chess is a game of strategy with a finite set of rules but an incredibly large number of possible moves. AI can play chess using algorithms that evaluate each possible move and predict the outcome of each one. Early AI systems used brute-force **search algorithms** to evaluate every possible move. These systems were able to analyze many moves ahead of time, looking for the most advantageous outcome.

- o **Minimax Algorithm**: The **Minimax** algorithm is one of the most popular search algorithms used in chess. It explores the game tree (all possible moves) and assigns a value to each node (each possible position in the game). The AI looks for moves that maximize its advantage while minimizing the opponent's options.

- o **Example**: In a chess game, if the AI evaluates the board and sees that a particular move would lead to a checkmate in 3 turns, it will choose that move. It also evaluates counter-moves by the opponent to ensure that the move will not result in a loss.

2. **AI in Modern Chess**: Modern chess engines, such as **Stockfish** and **AlphaZero**, go beyond simple search algorithms and utilize more advanced techniques like **neural networks** to evaluate board positions. **AlphaZero**, developed by Google's DeepMind, used a form of **reinforcement learning** to learn how to play chess at a superhuman level. After playing millions of games against itself, AlphaZero became capable of discovering novel strategies that even experienced human players had not considered.

- o **Example**: In 2017, AlphaZero defeated Stockfish (one of the strongest chess engines) by using reinforcement learning. Unlike traditional chess engines, AlphaZero was not pre-programmed with any chess knowledge. It learned purely through self-play and neural networks, showcasing how AI can evolve problem-solving strategies autonomously.

3. **Games as a Problem-Solving Environment**: Games like chess, Go, or even puzzles like Sudoku provide ideal environments for testing AI's problem-solving abilities. They present a clear set of rules, a large number of possible states, and the need for strategic decision-making, making them excellent benchmarks for AI performance.

   o **Example**: **DeepMind's AlphaGo** used a combination of deep learning and reinforcement learning to master the ancient game of Go. Unlike chess, Go has an exponentially larger game tree, making it much more difficult for traditional search algorithms to evaluate all possible moves. AlphaGo's ability to outplay world champions in Go demonstrated how advanced AI can solve incredibly complex problems.

In this chapter, we've explored the central role of **algorithms** in AI systems and how they enable machines to solve problems. We examined various problem-solving methods used in AI, such as search algorithms, heuristics, optimization algorithms, and rule-based systems. These methods allow AI to process information, analyze potential solutions, and choose the most appropriate action. We also looked at how AI solves complex problems in puzzles and games, with examples like **chess** and **Go** demonstrating how AI can evaluate and predict outcomes to make strategic decisions.

By understanding the algorithms and methods that power AI, it's easier to see how these systems function and learn over time, transforming data into actionable knowledge.

# CHAPTER 5: DATA: THE FUEL FOR AI

### *Importance of Data in AI Development*

Data is the most crucial resource for any AI system. Without data, an AI system cannot learn, improve, or make informed decisions. In fact, the phrase **"data is the new oil"** has become widely used to emphasize its centrality in AI development. The more high-quality data an AI system is exposed to, the better it can perform in tasks like predictions, classifications, and decision-making.

Here's why data is vital:

1. **Training AI Models**: In machine learning, AI models are trained using large datasets. These datasets provide the examples the AI needs to learn patterns, relationships, and characteristics that enable it to make predictions or perform tasks. For instance, an AI trained to recognize images of cats needs thousands of labeled images (data) showing cats in various settings, lighting, and poses to identify new cat images accurately.

2. **Improving AI Performance**: The more diverse and extensive the data, the more effective and adaptable an AI model becomes. Real-world data includes noise, variation, and complexity, so the quality and quantity of the data can directly affect how well an AI system generalizes to new, unseen data. This is why large companies like Google, Amazon, and Facebook collect massive amounts of data to continually improve their AI systems.

3. **Refinement through Feedback**: Once an AI system is deployed, it requires continuous feedback in the form of new data to maintain its relevance. For instance, a recommendation engine on Netflix needs up-to-date user interaction data to suggest new movies based on recent viewing preferences.

4. **Real-World Applications**: From healthcare to finance, AI systems rely on data to solve real-world problems. For example, AI is used in medical diagnostics by analyzing

vast amounts of patient data and medical records to predict diseases or suggest treatments. In finance, AI analyzes transaction data to detect fraud or predict stock market trends.

## Data Types: Structured vs. Unstructured

In AI, data is often categorized into two broad types: **structured data** and **unstructured data**. These categories reflect how data is organized and the complexity involved in processing it.

1. **Structured Data**: Structured data refers to data that is highly organized and formatted in a way that is easy to process. This type of data is typically stored in tables with rows and columns (like in databases or spreadsheets). It follows a strict schema or format, making it easy for machines to interpret and analyze.

   o **Characteristics**:
   - Organized into rows, columns, and fields
   - Easy to process and analyze using traditional data processing tools
   - Examples: Numbers, dates, customer names, transaction amounts, etc.

   o **Example**: A **customer database** where each row represents a different customer, and columns include fields like name, age, address, and purchase history. Structured data is ideal for performing statistical analysis or feeding into machine learning algorithms like decision trees or linear regression.

- o **Real-World Application**: A **bank's transaction history** is structured data, where each transaction is logged with precise details like date, amount, and the accounts involved. AI systems can analyze these logs to detect unusual patterns or potential fraudulent activities.

2. **Unstructured Data**: Unstructured data is the opposite of structured data. It does not have a predefined structure or format, which makes it more complex to process. This type of data can include text, images, audio, and video, and it requires more sophisticated AI techniques, such as natural language processing (NLP) or computer vision, to extract meaningful insights.

- o **Characteristics**:
  - Not organized in a specific format
  - Requires advanced techniques (e.g., deep learning) for interpretation
  - Examples: Text documents, images, videos, social media posts, etc.

- o **Example**: **Customer reviews** on a website are unstructured data. The reviews may contain text in various forms—some might include sentiment (positive or negative), others may mention specific products or features. Analyzing this unstructured data requires NLP to interpret the meaning of the words and the sentiment behind them.

o **Real-World Application**: **Social media posts**, where people share opinions, images, and videos, are largely unstructured. AI systems use NLP to process and analyze text, and computer vision to analyze images, to gather insights such as public sentiment, trending topics, or potential marketing strategies.

3. **Semi-Structured Data**: In addition to fully structured and unstructured data, there is also **semi-structured data**. This type of data doesn't have a rigid structure like structured data, but it contains tags or markers that make it easier to analyze than purely unstructured data. Examples include **XML** files, **JSON** data, or emails.

o **Example**: An **email** is semi-structured because it has a consistent structure (e.g., sender, receiver, subject, date) but also contains body text, which is unstructured.

*Real-World Example: AI in Social Media Content Recommendation*

One of the most widespread uses of AI is in social media, where AI algorithms analyze data to personalize user experiences, specifically for content recommendation. Companies like Facebook, Instagram, and YouTube use AI to recommend posts, videos, and ads that align with a user's interests and behaviors.

Here's how AI works in social media content recommendation:

1. **Data Collection**: Social media platforms collect a massive amount of data about user interactions. This includes likes, shares, comments, watch history, search history, and even time spent on specific posts. Additionally, platforms track user demographics and behavioral data (location, device used, etc.). This data is typically a mix of **structured** (e.g., user profile data) and **unstructured** (e.g., text from comments, images, and video content).

2. **Algorithm Training**: AI uses this data to **train machine learning models** that predict the type of content users will engage with next. For example, when you "like" a post about fitness, the platform's algorithm learns about your interests and starts suggesting more fitness-related content in the future. It analyzes patterns in your behavior and compares it to the behavior of other users to make accurate predictions.

- **Structured Data**: The platform might use structured data, such as the time you spent watching videos, to gauge interest in certain types of content.
- **Unstructured Data**: AI algorithms also analyze unstructured data like the content of your comments, the captions in photos, and the tags in videos to assess your preferences and provide relevant recommendations.

3. **Personalization and Feedback Loop**: The more you interact with the content, the more the algorithm improves. If you watch a cooking tutorial or like a travel post, the AI model takes that feedback into account and adjusts the recommendations accordingly. This dynamic learning process allows AI to keep the content fresh and relevant to each individual user.

4. **Ethical Considerations**: While AI-driven recommendations improve user engagement, they also raise questions about **filter bubbles** (where users are only exposed to content that aligns with their existing views) and **data privacy**. Social media platforms must balance effective personalization with respecting user privacy and preventing echo chambers.

- **Example**: If you consistently watch videos on a specific political topic, the AI recommendation system might suggest more content on that same topic, potentially reinforcing existing biases. At the same time, data privacy concerns arise if too much personal information is used to tailor recommendations without proper consent.

---

In this chapter, we've seen that **data** is the fuel for AI development, powering machine learning models and algorithms that allow AI systems to perform tasks, make predictions, and solve problems. **Structured data**, such as numbers and text in databases, is easy for machines to process, while **unstructured data**, like images and social media content, requires more complex techniques to interpret. We also explored how AI uses both types of data to power **recommendation systems** on social media platforms, providing personalized content to users based on their behaviors and preferences. AI's ability to analyze

# CHAPTER 6: MACHINE LEARNING: THE HEART OF AI

*What is Machine Learning?*

**Machine learning (ML)** is a subset of AI that enables machines to learn from data and improve their performance over time without being explicitly programmed. In other words, instead of relying on predefined rules, ML algorithms identify patterns in data and use those patterns to make predictions, decisions, or classifications.

Machine learning involves creating models that learn from data inputs and can generalize this knowledge to unseen data. Unlike traditional programming, where humans dictate every step, machine learning empowers systems to learn autonomously from experiences.

There are three primary types of machine learning:

1. **Supervised Learning**: In supervised learning, the machine is trained on labeled data—data that includes both inputs and their corresponding outputs. The goal is for the machine to learn the relationship between inputs and outputs so that it can predict the output for new, unseen inputs.

   o **Example**: If you're teaching a machine to recognize handwritten digits, the algorithm is given thousands of images of handwritten digits labeled with the correct numbers (e.g., "3," "7," "9"). It learns the features of each digit and can later identify digits in new images.

2. **Unsupervised Learning**: In unsupervised learning, the machine is given data without labels, meaning it has to find patterns, correlations, or structures within the data on its own. This type of learning is used to identify hidden patterns or groupings in data.

o **Example**: Unsupervised learning is used in clustering, where the algorithm groups similar data together. For instance, customer segmentation for marketing purposes might use unsupervised learning to group customers based on buying behavior.

3. **Reinforcement Learning**: Reinforcement learning involves an agent that learns by interacting with an environment and receiving feedback through rewards or penalties based on its actions. The system learns to optimize its behavior to achieve the most favorable outcome.

o **Example**: A robot learning to navigate a maze, receiving positive feedback when it moves closer to the exit and negative feedback when it hits a wall.

---

### How Machines "Learn" from Data

Machine learning involves training a model on data and using that model to make decisions or predictions. Here's a step-by-step breakdown of how machines learn from data:

1. **Data Collection**: The first step in machine learning is gathering data. This can include historical data, user behavior data, sensor data, and much more. The quality and

quantity of the data directly impact the model's performance.

- o **Example**: To build a machine learning model to detect spam emails, the model needs a large dataset of emails labeled as "spam" or "not spam."

2. **Preprocessing and Feature Engineering**: Once the data is collected, it needs to be cleaned and prepared for training. This includes removing irrelevant or redundant data, handling missing values, and transforming the data into a format that the machine learning algorithm can process.

Feature engineering is also an essential part of this process. It involves selecting and creating the most relevant features (attributes or variables) in the data to help the model make more accurate predictions.

- o **Example**: In the case of spam email detection, features might include the presence of certain keywords (e.g., "win money," "urgent") or the sender's email address.

3. **Training the Model**: The machine learning algorithm is then trained on the preprocessed data. During training, the algorithm adjusts its internal parameters (often called "weights" in models like neural networks) to minimize the error between its predictions and the true outputs (labels).

o **Example**: For supervised learning, the algorithm learns by comparing its predictions of "spam" vs. "not spam" to the actual labels and adjusts accordingly to improve accuracy.

4. **Model Evaluation**: After training, the model is tested on new, unseen data (called a validation or test set). This is done to evaluate how well the model generalizes to new data. Common evaluation metrics include accuracy, precision, recall, and F1-score.

   o **Example**: If the spam filter model correctly identifies 90% of the spam emails and misses 10%, the evaluation helps determine if the model needs further refinement.

5. **Prediction/Inference**: After training and evaluation, the model can be used to make predictions on new, unseen data. The machine will apply the patterns it learned during training to predict the outcome for future inputs.

   o **Example**: Once the spam filter is trained, it can automatically classify new incoming emails as either spam or not spam.

6. **Improvement through Feedback**: Over time, machine learning models can continue to improve through feedback. This is often done through continuous retraining using new data or by fine-tuning the model's parameters to optimize performance.

o **Example**: If a spam filter starts to miss new types of spam emails (e.g., from a new sender or with new wording), the system can learn from this feedback and improve its detection in future instances.

---

## Example: Spam Filters in Email

One of the most common applications of machine learning in everyday life is **spam filtering** in email. A spam filter uses machine learning to identify unsolicited or harmful emails (spam) and prevent them from appearing in your inbox. Here's how the process works:

1. **Data Collection**: To build a spam filter, you need a large dataset of emails that are labeled as either **spam** or **not spam** (often called "ham"). These labels are provided either manually or through a curated database of known spam emails.

2. **Preprocessing**: The emails in the dataset are preprocessed. This might involve removing email headers (like the "From" field), converting the text to lowercase, and tokenizing the email body into individual words or phrases.

   Feature extraction might also be done at this stage, such as identifying whether certain words or patterns commonly appear in spam emails (e.g., "free money," "limited time offer").

3. **Training**: The spam filter uses **supervised learning** to train on the dataset. The algorithm learns to associate certain features of the emails with their labels (spam or not spam). For example, it might learn that emails with phrases like "win a free iPhone" or "buy now" are more likely to be spam.

4. **Evaluation**: The model is then tested on new emails (a separate validation set) to evaluate how accurately it can classify spam vs. non-spam emails. It may get evaluated based on accuracy (correct predictions) or precision/recall (how many spam emails it catches vs. how many it misses).

5. **Prediction/Inference**: Once trained and evaluated, the spam filter is ready to be deployed. As new emails arrive in your inbox, the filter classifies them as either spam or not spam based on the patterns it has learned.

   o **Example**: An email from an unknown sender with the subject "Congratulations! You've won a free vacation!" might be classified as spam, while an email from a trusted colleague would be classified as not spam.

6. **Improvement**: Over time, the spam filter can continue to improve. If users mark an email as spam (or not spam), that feedback can be used to retrain the model, refining its

ability to classify emails more accurately. This allows the filter to adapt to new kinds of spam tactics.

---

In this chapter, we explored **machine learning**, the heart of AI, and how it enables machines to learn from data and improve over time. We examined the machine learning process—from collecting and preparing data, to training models, to making predictions and continuously improving. We also looked at a real-world example of machine learning in action: **spam filters** in email. By learning from labeled data (spam or not spam), the spam filter can classify new emails accurately, and continuously improve based on user feedback. This ability of machines to learn from data is what makes machine learning such a powerful tool for solving a wide variety of problems in AI.

# CHAPTER 7: SUPERVISED LEARNING: TEACHING WITH LABELS

## How Supervised Learning Works

**Supervised learning** is one of the most commonly used types of machine learning. In this method, an AI system is trained using **labeled data**, which means the data includes both the input (features) and the corresponding correct output (label). The goal of supervised learning is for the machine to learn the mapping between inputs and outputs so it can predict the correct output when given new, unseen data.

The supervised learning process involves the following key steps:

1. **Data Collection**: To begin, you collect a dataset that includes both **input features** and the **target labels**. For example, if you're building a model to predict house prices, your dataset would include features like square footage, location, number of bedrooms, etc., and the corresponding labels would be the actual sale price of those houses.

2. **Training**: During training, the algorithm is fed labeled data and learns by comparing its predictions with the correct answers (labels). The model adjusts its internal parameters to reduce the difference between its predictions and the actual labels. This process is typically done using optimization algorithms like **gradient descent**.

   o **Example**: In the case of predicting house prices, the machine will learn how different features (such as the number of bedrooms, location, and size) correlate with the price of a house.

3. **Model Evaluation**: After training, the model is tested on new, unseen data (validation or test data) to check its performance. The model's ability to make accurate predictions on the test set is key to determining whether the model is generalizing well to new data or simply memorizing the training data (a problem known as overfitting).

4. **Prediction**: Once the model is trained and evaluated, it can be used to make predictions on new data. Given new input features (like the size of a house, number of rooms, etc.), the model will predict the output (in this case, the house price).

   o **Example**: The trained model could predict the price of a house not in the training data based on its features, like location and size.

5. **Continuous Learning**: In some cases, supervised learning models can continue to improve over time. If more labeled data is collected or if the model's predictions are refined with new information, the model can be retrained to improve its accuracy.

*Training AI with Labeled Data*

In supervised learning, labeled data is crucial for teaching the machine how to make predictions. Labeled data consists of **input-output pairs**, where each input is a feature or set of features, and the output is the label or target value.

1. **Input Features**: These are the characteristics or attributes that describe the data points. For example, in a dataset of houses, the input features could include **square footage**, **number of bedrooms**, **location**, **age of the house**, etc.
2. **Labels**: The label is the target value the AI is trying to predict. In the house price prediction example, the label would be the **sale price** of each house.
3. **Training the Model**: When a model is trained on labeled data, it attempts to learn the relationship between the features (inputs) and the labels (outputs). The model adjusts its internal parameters to minimize the error in its predictions, typically by using an optimization technique like **gradient descent**.
   - **Example**: If the model predicts a house price that is too high, it will adjust its parameters to lower the prediction, and vice versa. Over time, it will learn the best set of parameters to predict house prices as accurately as possible.
4. **Data Quality**: The quality of labeled data is critical. If the data is noisy, inconsistent, or contains errors, the model's performance will suffer. Data preprocessing techniques,

such as handling missing values, removing outliers, and normalizing features, are often used to ensure the quality of labeled data.

---

### *Real-World Example: Predicting House Prices Based on Historical Data*

A classic example of supervised learning in action is predicting **house prices** based on historical data. Here's how it works step by step:

1. **Data Collection**: To predict house prices, you gather historical data about homes that have already been sold. The dataset could include various features (inputs) of the homes, such as:
   - **Square footage**: The size of the house (in square feet).
   - **Number of bedrooms**: The number of bedrooms in the house.
   - **Location**: The neighborhood or area where the house is located.
   - **Age of the house**: How old the property is.
   - **Lot size**: The size of the land the house is built on.

The corresponding labels in this dataset would be the **sale prices** of the houses, i.e., the target value the model is trying to predict.

2. **Data Preprocessing**: Once the data is collected, it needs to be cleaned and prepared for the machine learning algorithm. This might involve:

    o Handling missing data (e.g., filling in missing values or removing incomplete rows).

    o Encoding categorical variables (e.g., converting "location" into a numerical value representing different neighborhoods).

    o Normalizing the data to ensure that features like square footage and lot size are on the same scale, making it easier for the algorithm to learn patterns.

3. **Training the Model**: With the cleaned and preprocessed data, a supervised learning algorithm (such as **linear regression**, **decision trees**, or **random forests**) is trained on the dataset. The model learns the relationship between the features (like square footage, number of bedrooms) and the price of the house.

During training, the model will adjust its parameters to minimize the difference between the predicted prices and the actual sale prices. For example, the model might learn that houses with more square footage tend to have higher prices, or that homes in certain neighborhoods are more expensive.

4. **Model Evaluation**: After training, the model is evaluated using a separate validation or test dataset (i.e., a set of houses it hasn't seen before). The model's predictions are compared to the actual prices, and metrics like **mean absolute error (MAE)** or **mean squared error (MSE)** are used to evaluate its accuracy.

   o **Example**: If the model predicts the price of a house to be $300,000, but the actual price was $320,000, the error would be $20,000.

5. **Prediction**: Once the model is trained and validated, it can be used to predict the price of a new house based on its features. For instance, if a new house has 2,000 square feet, 3 bedrooms, and is located in a certain neighborhood, the model can predict its sale price.

   o **Example**: Given the features of a new house, the model might predict its price to be $350,000 based on the patterns it has learned from the historical data.

6. **Improvement**: As more data becomes available (e.g., new house sales), the model can be retrained to improve its accuracy and adapt to changes in the housing market.

In this chapter, we've explored **supervised learning**, a fundamental method of machine learning where AI is trained on labeled data. Supervised learning allows machines to learn the relationship between input features (like square footage, number of bedrooms, and location) and target labels (such as house prices). Through training, the model adjusts its parameters to predict the label accurately when given new data. The example of **predicting house prices** illustrates how supervised learning works in practice, with the model learning from historical data and making predictions about future house sales.

# CHAPTER 8: UNSUPERVISED LEARNING: LETTING AI DISCOVER PATTERNS

*What is Unsupervised Learning?*

**Unsupervised learning** is a type of machine learning where the model is trained on **unlabeled data**—data that does not include predefined outputs or labels. The goal of unsupervised learning is to let the algorithm discover hidden patterns or structures within the data on its own, without human intervention or supervision.

In supervised learning, we provide the algorithm with labeled data (inputs paired with the correct outputs), but in unsupervised learning, the algorithm is given only the inputs and must find its own way to make sense of the data. This makes unsupervised learning especially useful when labeled data is difficult, expensive, or time-consuming to obtain.

Unsupervised learning is typically used for tasks like clustering, anomaly detection, and association, where the aim is to understand the underlying structure of the data rather than predict specific outcomes.

### *How AI Finds Patterns Without Labeled Data*

Since unsupervised learning uses data that is not labeled, the model must find patterns or relationships in the data without predefined outcomes. Here's how unsupervised learning works:

1. **Data Collection**: The first step is to gather a dataset, just like in supervised learning. However, in unsupervised learning, the dataset only contains the **input features**—no output labels. For instance, you might have a set of customer data that includes features such as age, income, and purchase history, but you won't have any predefined labels for whether a customer belongs to a certain group or category.

2. **Pattern Discovery**: The unsupervised learning algorithm then begins to analyze the data and attempts to find hidden patterns or relationships. The algorithm may look for clusters of data points that are similar to each other (this is called **clustering**), detect anomalies (called **outlier detection**), or identify associations between features (known as **association rule learning**).

   o **Example**: If you have customer data that includes age and income, the algorithm might discover that there are distinct groups of customers, such as one group of young, high-income customers and another group of older, lower-income customers.

3. **Clustering**: One of the most common methods used in unsupervised learning is **clustering**, where the algorithm groups similar data points together into clusters. Clustering algorithms work by measuring the similarity between data points (often using distance metrics like Euclidean distance) and grouping those that are closest to each other into a cluster.

   o **Example**: A clustering algorithm might group customers into different segments based on their purchasing behavior. One group might be frequent shoppers, while another might make occasional, high-value purchases.

4. **Dimensionality Reduction**: Another common technique in unsupervised learning is **dimensionality reduction**, where the algorithm simplifies the data by reducing the number of features or variables while preserving the most important information. This can help reveal patterns that may be obscured by too many features.

   o **Example**: In customer data with many attributes (e.g., age, income, location, product preferences, etc.), dimensionality reduction techniques like **Principal Component Analysis (PCA)** can reduce the data to a few key dimensions that still capture the most important aspects of the data.

5. **Self-Organizing**: Unsupervised learning algorithms, especially clustering models like **k-means clustering** or **hierarchical clustering**, aim to self-organize the data into meaningful categories or groups. The model iteratively adjusts its structure, refining its understanding of the patterns in the data until it reaches the optimal grouping or structure.

---

### *Real-World Example: Customer Segmentation for Marketing*

One of the most powerful and common applications of unsupervised learning is **customer segmentation**. This process involves dividing customers into distinct groups based on shared characteristics, allowing businesses to tailor their marketing efforts more effectively. Since companies often have large amounts of customer data but lack predefined categories (such as the best target demographic for a new product), unsupervised learning becomes a critical tool.

Here's how unsupervised learning can be used for **customer segmentation**:

1. **Data Collection**: To segment customers, a company would gather a dataset that includes relevant customer information. This data might include:

- o **Demographic data**: Age, gender, income, education level, etc.
- o **Behavioral data**: Purchase history, frequency of visits, preferred products, etc.
- o **Engagement data**: Interactions with emails, website clicks, social media engagement, etc.

The data does not come with any labels, meaning the company doesn't know in advance which customers should be grouped together.

2. **Clustering**: An unsupervised learning algorithm (e.g., **k-means clustering** or **DBSCAN**) is applied to this data. The algorithm analyzes the features of the customers and groups them based on similarity. For instance, the algorithm might identify that customers aged 18-30 with high social media engagement and frequent online purchases belong to one group, while customers aged 50-60 who make fewer purchases but tend to buy in bulk belong to another.

3. **Pattern Discovery**: The clustering algorithm may identify interesting patterns that businesses might not have considered. For example, it might find that younger customers tend to prefer eco-friendly products, while older customers are more price-sensitive. These patterns can help the business refine its marketing strategies.

4. **Actionable Insights**: The business can now tailor its marketing campaigns to the specific segments identified by the unsupervised learning algorithm. For example:

   o For the eco-conscious younger segment, the company might promote new sustainable products via social media platforms.

   o For the older, price-sensitive group, the company could send targeted discounts via email or offer bulk purchasing incentives.

5. **Ongoing Refinement**: As new customer data is collected (e.g., after a marketing campaign or product launch), the segmentation model can be retrained or refined, ensuring that the segmentation remains relevant and up-to-date.

In this chapter, we've explored **unsupervised learning**, a type of machine learning that allows AI systems to find patterns in unlabeled data. Unlike supervised learning, which relies on labeled data, unsupervised learning enables AI to discover hidden structures or groupings within the data. We looked at how unsupervised learning can be applied to real-world problems like **customer segmentation** in marketing. By clustering customers based on shared features such as purchasing behavior or demographic data, businesses can tailor their marketing efforts more effectively. Unsupervised learning plays a crucial role in identifying patterns and insights that may not be immediately obvious, making it a powerful tool for data-driven decision-making.

# CHAPTER 9: REINFORCEMENT LEARNING: AI LEARNING THROUGH FEEDBACK

*Explanation of Reinforcement Learning*

**Reinforcement Learning (RL)** is a type of machine learning where an agent learns to make decisions by interacting with an environment and receiving feedback in the form of **rewards** or **punishments** based on its actions. Unlike supervised learning, where the model is trained with labeled data, reinforcement learning focuses on **trial and error**, where the agent tries different actions, learns from the results, and gradually improves its decision-making strategy to maximize cumulative rewards.

In RL, there are three primary components that define the learning process:

1.  **Agent**: The learner or decision-maker (e.g., a robot, a video game character, or an autonomous vehicle).

2.  **Environment**: The surroundings with which the agent interacts. The environment provides feedback (rewards or penalties) based on the actions taken by the agent.

3.  **Action**: The decisions or moves made by the agent within the environment. Each action leads to a new state in the environment.

4.  **Reward**: The feedback received from the environment after an action is taken. The reward is a scalar value, which can be positive (for a good action) or negative (for a bad action). The goal is to maximize the total reward over time.

5.  **State**: A description of the current situation or configuration of the environment.

6.  **Policy**: A strategy or mapping from states to actions, guiding the agent's decisions. The goal is for the agent to learn the best policy that maximizes its long-term reward.

Reinforcement learning can be contrasted with supervised learning, where a model is trained on a dataset with predefined labels. In RL, the agent doesn't know the "correct answer" in advance and must explore different actions and states to figure out the best strategy.

*AI Learning Through Trial and Error*

The key idea behind reinforcement learning is that an agent learns from **trial and error**. Instead of being given correct answers, the agent must explore its environment, take actions, and receive feedback. Here's how it works in more detail:

1. **Exploration**: Initially, the agent is unsure about which actions lead to the best outcomes, so it tries a variety of actions. This phase is known as **exploration**. The agent takes random actions in different states of the environment to gather data and learn from its experiences.

2. **Exploitation**: As the agent explores and learns from the environment, it begins to exploit the knowledge it has gained. **Exploitation** refers to choosing actions that the agent has learned will lead to the best possible rewards based on past experiences.

3. **Balancing Exploration and Exploitation**: One of the key challenges in reinforcement learning is balancing **exploration** (trying new actions) and **exploitation** (choosing the best-known action). If the agent only exploits known actions, it might miss discovering better strategies, but if it only explores, it may never settle on an optimal solution.

4. **Learning from Feedback**: After each action, the agent receives feedback in the form of rewards or penalties. Over time, the agent uses this feedback to adjust its strategy and improve its future actions. The agent's ultimate goal is to

maximize its cumulative reward over time, often referred to as the **return**.

5. **Value Function**: The agent learns to estimate the **value** of a state or action based on the expected future reward it will receive from that state or action. The value function helps the agent decide which actions to take in a given state.

   o **Example**: In a maze, the agent might calculate the value of being at a certain location based on how close it is to the exit. The agent will prefer to take actions that lead it toward the exit and avoid those that move it away from it.

---

## Example: AI Playing Video Games (e.g., AlphaGo)

One of the most famous applications of reinforcement learning is in the development of AI systems that can play complex games like **AlphaGo**. Let's explore how reinforcement learning works in this context:

1. **The Game Environment**: In video games or board games, the game environment provides the agent (the AI) with a set of rules that govern how the game is played. The agent interacts with this environment by choosing actions (e.g., moving a piece on a board, or in the case of video games, controlling a character) to progress in the game.

2. **Trial and Error**: Initially, the AI has no idea how to play the game, so it explores different strategies by trying out random actions. At first, the AI's moves might seem ineffective or even counterproductive, but through **trial and error**, it starts to identify which actions lead to winning outcomes.

   o **Example**: In **AlphaGo**, the AI would play thousands (or millions) of games, initially using random strategies, but then learning which strategies led to victories and which led to losses. Through this process, it learns the long-term rewards associated with each move in the game of Go.

3. **Rewards and Feedback**: After each action, the AI receives feedback. For instance, in **AlphaGo**, the AI was rewarded for capturing pieces and securing a victory, while it was penalized for losing pieces or making poor moves. Over time, this feedback helps the AI understand which moves contribute to winning and which don't.

4. **Learning and Refining the Strategy**: After many iterations of trial and error, the AI learns to predict which actions will lead to the best outcomes. The agent refines its strategy by using **reinforcement signals** to maximize the expected reward. In AlphaGo's case, this meant mastering

complex strategies and evaluating positions on the board with incredible precision.

5. **AlphaGo's Success**: AlphaGo's success is a prime example of reinforcement learning's power. AlphaGo famously defeated the world champion in Go, a game much more complex than chess due to the larger board size and more possible moves. It did so by combining **deep neural networks** and **Monte Carlo tree search** with reinforcement learning, where the system learned from millions of games played against itself.

   o **Example**: In a Go match, AlphaGo would evaluate different positions and moves in real-time, using its learned strategy to predict the most likely path to victory. Through this, it was able to develop strategies that even human experts had never considered.

In this chapter, we've explored **reinforcement learning (RL)**, a type of machine learning where AI agents learn to make decisions through trial and error. Reinforcement learning involves an agent interacting with an environment, taking actions, and receiving feedback in the form of rewards or penalties. The agent's goal is to maximize the total reward over time by finding the best strategies for each situation. We discussed how **AlphaGo**, the AI that defeated world champions in the complex game of Go, is an example of RL in action, where the AI learned optimal strategies by playing millions of games and refining its approach. This ability to learn through feedback makes reinforcement learning a powerful method for training AI to handle complex, dynamic environments like video games, robotics, and autonomous systems.

# CHAPTER 10: NEURAL NETWORKS: MIMICKING THE HUMAN BRAIN

## *Introduction to Neural Networks*

A **neural network** is a machine learning model inspired by the structure and function of the human brain. Just as the brain processes information through interconnected neurons, a neural network consists of layers of **artificial neurons** (also called nodes or units) that work together to solve tasks like classification, prediction, and pattern recognition.

Neural networks are a key component of **deep learning**, a subset of machine learning that excels in handling complex tasks involving large amounts of data, such as image recognition, natural language processing, and speech recognition.

The basic idea of a neural network is to simulate the way biological brains process and learn from information, but in a mathematical and computational form. Neural networks are particularly powerful because they can learn from data by adjusting the strength (or "weight") of the connections between neurons during training. This enables them to automatically learn patterns and representations from raw data, without requiring hand-crafted features or explicit programming for every task.

---

### *How Neural Networks Simulate the Brain's Structure*

The structure of a neural network is inspired by the human brain, but it is simpler and more abstract. Here's a breakdown of the key components:

1. **Neurons**:
   - **Biological Brain**: In the human brain, neurons are cells that transmit electrical signals. Neurons are connected to one another through synapses, and each neuron processes information based on its inputs and passes it on to other neurons.
   - **Artificial Neurons**: In a neural network, artificial neurons are simple computational units that take input data, process it, and produce an output. Each neuron receives inputs, applies a weight to each input, and passes the weighted sum through an activation function to produce an output.
2. **Layers of Neurons**:

- o A neural network typically consists of multiple layers of neurons:
  - **Input Layer**: This is the first layer, which receives the raw data. Each neuron in the input layer represents a feature of the data. For example, in image recognition, each input neuron might represent a pixel value in an image.
  - **Hidden Layers**: These intermediate layers perform most of the computation. Each hidden layer processes the inputs it receives and passes its output to the next layer. In deep learning, networks can have many hidden layers, allowing them to learn increasingly abstract and complex representations of the data.
  - **Output Layer**: This final layer provides the network's prediction or classification result. For example, in a binary classification task, the output layer would indicate whether an image is a cat or a dog.

3. **Connections and Weights**:
   - o Just as neurons in the brain are connected by synapses, artificial neurons are connected by **weights**. These weights control the strength of the

connection between neurons and determine how much influence one neuron has on another.

○ During training, the neural network adjusts these weights to minimize errors and improve its predictions. This process is known as **training** and is typically done using algorithms like **backpropagation** and **gradient descent**.

4. **Activation Function**:

○ Each neuron in a neural network applies an **activation function** to the weighted sum of its inputs. The activation function determines whether a neuron "fires" and passes its signal on to the next layer. Common activation functions include **sigmoid, tanh**, and **ReLU (Rectified Linear Unit)**.

○ The activation function helps introduce non-linearity into the network, enabling it to learn complex patterns in the data.

5. **Learning Through Backpropagation**:

○ Neural networks learn by adjusting the weights of the connections between neurons to minimize the error in their predictions. This is done using a method called **backpropagation**, where the network computes the gradient of the error with respect to the weights and adjusts the weights in the direction that reduces the error. This process is repeated over many iterations (epochs) until the network achieves good performance.

---

*Real-World Example: AI Recognizing Images (e.g., Facial Recognition)*

One of the most powerful applications of neural networks is **image recognition**, where the network is trained to identify objects, faces, or scenes in images. A common example is **facial recognition**, where a neural network is used to identify or verify individuals based on their facial features.

Here's how neural networks are used in facial recognition:

1. **Data Collection**: To train a neural network for facial recognition, a large dataset of labeled images is required. Each image in the dataset is labeled with the identity of the person in the image. These images may come from different angles, lighting conditions, and facial expressions to help the network learn to generalize well across various conditions.

2. **Preprocessing**: Before feeding the images into the neural network, the data is often preprocessed. This could include resizing the images to a standard size, converting them to grayscale (if color is not important), and normalizing the pixel values to fall within a specific range.

3. **Input Layer**: The input layer of the neural network receives the raw image data. In the case of facial recognition, each pixel in the image might be represented as an input feature. For example, if an image is 100x100 pixels, the input layer could consist of 10,000 neurons (one for each pixel).

4. **Hidden Layers**: The hidden layers of the network process the input data and learn increasingly complex features of the image. In early layers, the network might learn simple features like edges and corners. In deeper layers, the network learns more abstract features like shapes, textures, and patterns that help identify specific facial characteristics.

5. **Output Layer**: The output layer of the network generates a prediction. For facial recognition, the output might be a classification of the person in the image, or a probability score indicating how likely it is that the person in the image matches a known individual.

6. **Training the Network**: During training, the neural network uses labeled images to learn the mapping between the image features and the identity of the person. The network adjusts its weights through backpropagation, iteratively improving its ability to recognize faces. The more data the network is exposed to, the better it can generalize to new, unseen faces.

7. **Real-World Use**: Once the neural network is trained, it can be deployed in real-world applications, such as:

   o **Security Systems**: Identifying individuals in surveillance footage or granting access to secure locations based on facial recognition.

   o **Social Media**: Automatically tagging individuals in photos on platforms like Facebook or Instagram.

   o **Smartphones**: Unlocking devices using facial recognition for authentication (e.g., Apple's Face ID).

   o **Example**: In **Apple's Face ID**, the neural network on the iPhone uses advanced algorithms to process the user's facial features and compare them to the stored template to verify identity. The network can handle variations in lighting, angles, and facial expressions, making it a robust and accurate authentication method.

8. **Challenges**: While neural networks have become highly effective at facial recognition, they are not without challenges. Issues such as bias in training data, security concerns (e.g., spoofing), and privacy implications are important considerations when deploying facial recognition systems.

In this chapter, we introduced **neural networks**, a powerful class of machine learning models inspired by the human brain. Neural networks consist of layers of artificial neurons that process input data, adjust their weights through training, and make predictions or classifications. These networks are particularly effective in tasks that require learning complex patterns, such as **image recognition**. We explored how neural networks are used in **facial recognition**, where they learn to identify individuals by processing facial features in images. Neural networks have become a cornerstone of deep learning applications and continue to drive advancements in fields like computer vision, natural language processing, and autonomous systems.

# CHAPTER 11: DEEP LEARNING: A STEP BEYOND NEURAL NETWORKS

---

## *What is Deep Learning?*

**Deep learning** is a subset of machine learning that focuses on using multi-layered **neural networks** to model and solve complex problems. While traditional neural networks are typically composed of just one or two layers of artificial neurons, deep learning networks, also known as **deep neural networks (DNNs)**, consist of many layers—hence the term "deep."

Deep learning has gained tremendous popularity due to its ability to handle large, high-dimensional datasets and learn intricate patterns in data without the need for manual feature engineering. This makes it particularly effective in solving tasks like image and speech recognition, natural language processing, and autonomous driving.

Deep learning algorithms are built on the foundation of neural networks but take advantage of **multiple hidden layers** that allow the model to learn progressively more complex features from the input data.

---

### *How Deep Learning Uses Multiple Layers for Complex Tasks*

Deep learning models are characterized by their use of multiple layers of artificial neurons. Each layer in a deep network transforms the data in ways that increase in complexity as it moves through the layers. This hierarchical learning structure allows the model to learn abstract features from raw data, leading to powerful predictions and insights.

1. **Layered Architecture**: Deep learning networks are made up of three types of layers:
   - **Input Layer**: The first layer that receives the raw data. For instance, in image recognition, each neuron in the input layer might correspond to one pixel in the image.
   - **Hidden Layers**: The core of deep learning. These intermediate layers process the data in increasingly

abstract ways. Each layer extracts different features of the input data, from simple to complex.

o **Output Layer**: The final layer that provides the prediction or classification result. For instance, in an image classification task, the output layer would indicate the predicted label (e.g., "cat" or "dog").

2. **Feature Hierarchy**: As data passes through each layer, the network learns more sophisticated representations of the input data. Early layers might learn to detect basic features like edges or textures in images. As the data moves deeper through the network, the layers combine these simple features into more complex structures like shapes, objects, or faces.

o **Example**: In a **face recognition** model, the first layers may detect edges or colors, the middle layers might detect facial features like eyes or noses, and the deeper layers would recognize specific faces.

3. **Training with Backpropagation**: Deep learning models are trained using a technique called **backpropagation**, which adjusts the weights of the connections between neurons to minimize prediction errors. The network processes input data through the layers, makes a prediction, compares it to the actual output, and adjusts the weights accordingly to reduce the error. This process is repeated over many iterations to refine the model's performance.

4. **Activation Functions**: Each neuron in a deep network uses an **activation function** to process its inputs. These functions introduce non-linearity into the network, which allows it to learn complex patterns. Common activation functions used in deep learning include **ReLU (Rectified Linear Unit), sigmoid**, and **tanh**.

---

## *Example: AI in Self-Driving Cars*

One of the most compelling applications of deep learning is in **self-driving cars**, where AI is responsible for interpreting sensor data, making real-time decisions, and controlling the vehicle. Deep learning models are used to help self-driving cars "see" and understand their environment, make decisions like when to stop or turn, and navigate safely without human intervention.

Here's how deep learning plays a critical role in self-driving cars:

1. **Sensor Fusion and Input Data**: Self-driving cars rely on a variety of sensors, including **cameras, LiDAR** (Light Detection and Ranging), **radar**, and **ultrasonic sensors**, to gather data about their surroundings. The raw data from these sensors is fed into the deep learning network for processing.

   o **Cameras** provide visual information, capturing images of the car's surroundings.

o **LiDAR** and **radar** offer depth perception, helping the car detect the distance between objects in its environment.

o **Ultrasonic sensors** help with close-range sensing, useful for parking and avoiding obstacles.

This sensor data is processed by deep learning networks to detect and interpret various elements of the environment, such as pedestrians, other vehicles, traffic signs, and lane markings.

2. **Image and Object Recognition**: Deep learning models are used for **image classification** and **object detection**. For example, convolutional neural networks (**CNNs**), a specialized type of deep learning model, are well-suited for processing and recognizing patterns in visual data. CNNs break down the input image into smaller regions, learning to identify different objects or features, such as road signs, pedestrians, or other vehicles.

o **Example**: In a self-driving car, a deep learning network processes images from the car's cameras to detect a stop sign. The network's first layers may identify edges or shapes, the deeper layers might recognize the specific shape of the sign, and the final layers would classify the sign as a "stop sign."

3. **Decision-Making and Control**: Once the car's sensors have gathered and processed data about its environment, the deep learning system must decide what actions to take. This could involve detecting a pedestrian and applying the brakes, determining if it is safe to change lanes, or planning the best path through an intersection.

Deep reinforcement learning is often used in this context, where the car is trained to make decisions by interacting with a simulated driving environment. The system is rewarded for making safe, correct decisions and penalized for unsafe or incorrect actions. Over time, the car learns to navigate through complex environments, avoiding obstacles and following traffic rules.

   o **Example**: A self-driving car might encounter a pedestrian crossing the street. The deep learning system processes the data from the cameras and LiDAR to identify the pedestrian's position. Based on its learned experience, the car determines that the safest action is to slow down or stop to avoid hitting the pedestrian.

4. **End-to-End Learning**: Deep learning can enable **end-to-end learning**, where a neural network learns to control the entire self-driving system directly from raw input (e.g., camera images) to output actions (e.g., steering,

accelerating, or braking). This approach eliminates the need for explicit feature extraction or manual programming of driving rules.

- o **Example**: Companies like **Waymo** (a subsidiary of Alphabet) and **Tesla** use deep learning to process sensor data and make driving decisions in real-time, allowing the car to drive autonomously under most conditions.

5. **Challenges**: While deep learning has made great strides in self-driving technology, there are still challenges to address. For example:

- o **Edge cases**: Uncommon or rare situations that the AI has not been trained on, like unusual weather conditions or unpredictable pedestrian behavior.
- o **Safety**: Ensuring that the AI makes the right decision at every moment is critical, as errors could lead to accidents.
- o **Regulations and ethics**: Self-driving cars must comply with road laws and be designed to operate safely in a variety of environments and cultures.

---

In this chapter, we introduced **deep learning**, a powerful subset of machine learning that uses multi-layered neural networks to solve complex problems. Deep learning models are particularly adept at tasks like image and speech recognition because they can automatically learn hierarchical features from raw data through multiple layers of neurons. We also explored how deep learning is used in **self-driving cars**, where AI processes sensor data to recognize objects, make decisions, and navigate safely. By using deep neural networks, self-driving cars can interpret their surroundings and take actions like stopping for pedestrians or changing lanes, paving the way for autonomous transportation. Despite its successes, deep learning in autonomous vehicles still faces challenges like handling rare situations and ensuring safety, but it remains a critical component of the future of transportation.

# CHAPTER 12: NATURAL LANGUAGE PROCESSING (NLP): TEACHING MACHINES TO UNDERSTAND LANGUAGE

*What is NLP?*

**Natural Language Processing (NLP)** is a branch of artificial intelligence (AI) that focuses on the interaction between computers and human (natural) languages. The goal of NLP is to enable machines to understand, interpret, and generate human language in a way that is both meaningful and useful. This involves teaching computers to process and analyze large amounts of natural language data, such as written text or spoken speech.

NLP combines linguistics, computer science, and machine learning to enable computers to handle tasks involving human language. These tasks range from simple ones like word recognition to more complex ones like language translation or even understanding context and sentiment.

NLP is a crucial component of AI applications that interact with users through language, such as chatbots, virtual assistants, translation apps, and content recommendation systems. Its challenge lies in the ambiguity, complexity, and variety inherent in human language, as it can involve multiple meanings, sentence structures, and nuances.

---

### *Key Tasks in NLP*

NLP covers a wide range of tasks, each focused on different aspects of language. Here are some of the most common and important tasks in NLP:

1. **Text Classification**: Text classification is the task of assigning predefined labels or categories to text data. This can be used for various purposes, such as spam detection, sentiment analysis, or topic categorization.

- o **Example**: In email filtering, a text classification model might be used to categorize emails as **spam** or **not spam**. The model analyzes the content of the email and makes a prediction based on keywords, sentence structure, and other linguistic features.

- o **Applications**:
    - **Spam detection**: Classifying incoming emails as spam or not spam.
    - **Topic categorization**: Categorizing news articles into topics like politics, technology, or sports.

2. **Sentiment Analysis**: Sentiment analysis involves determining the emotional tone or sentiment of a piece of text. This task is useful in understanding opinions, reviews, or social media content. The goal is to classify the text as having positive, negative, or neutral sentiment.

    - o **Example**: In product reviews, sentiment analysis might be used to automatically determine whether a review is positive or negative. For instance, "This phone is amazing!" would be classified as positive, while "The battery life is terrible" would be negative.

    - o **Applications**:
        - **Customer feedback**: Analyzing reviews to gauge customer satisfaction.

- **Social media monitoring**: Understanding public sentiment towards brands or political events.

3. **Language Translation**: Language translation involves converting text from one language to another. Machine translation has been one of the most well-known applications of NLP, and it involves automatically translating text or speech from a source language to a target language.

   o **Example**: Tools like **Google Translate** use NLP algorithms to translate text or even whole sentences. For example, the sentence "How are you?" in English can be translated to "¿Cómo estás?" in Spanish.

   o **Applications**:

     - **Cross-lingual communication**: Translating documents, websites, or messages in real-time.

     - **Real-time conversation translation**: Tools like Skype Translator allow people speaking different languages to communicate in real-time by translating spoken language.

4. **Named Entity Recognition (NER)**: Named Entity Recognition is the process of identifying and classifying named entities in text, such as names of people,

organizations, dates, and locations. NER helps machines understand the meaning of specific terms and phrases in context.

- o **Example**: In the sentence "Apple Inc. announced its new iPhone model on October 12, 2023," NER would identify "Apple Inc." as an organization, "iPhone" as a product, and "October 12, 2023" as a date.

- o **Applications**:
    - **Information extraction**: Extracting key information from news articles or documents.
    - **Search engines**: Improving search results by identifying relevant entities in queries.

5. **Part-of-Speech Tagging**: Part-of-Speech (POS) tagging involves identifying the grammatical role of each word in a sentence, such as noun, verb, adjective, etc. This helps machines understand the structure of a sentence and interpret its meaning.

- o **Example**: In the sentence "The cat sat on the mat," a POS tagger would label "cat" as a noun, "sat" as a verb, and "on" as a preposition.

- o **Applications**:

- **Syntactic parsing**: Understanding sentence structure for tasks like question answering and information extraction.

- **Speech recognition**: Translating spoken language into text and understanding its meaning.

---

### *Real-World Example: Chatbots and Translation Apps*

1. **Chatbots**: Chatbots are AI-powered systems that simulate human conversation, typically through text or voice. They are commonly used in customer service, virtual assistants, and online support systems. Chatbots rely heavily on NLP to process user input, understand intent, and generate appropriate responses.

   o **How NLP is used**:

      - **Intent Recognition**: NLP algorithms help chatbots understand the user's intent behind their words. For example, if a user asks, "What's the weather like today?", the bot needs to recognize that the user is asking for weather information.

      - **Context Understanding**: Advanced chatbots use NLP to keep track of conversation context, making the dialogue flow naturally. For example, if a user says, "Show me the forecast for tomorrow," the bot understands that it should provide weather details for the next day.

- **Response Generation**: NLP models generate responses based on the input and context. The bot might use pre-defined templates or generate new responses using language generation models.

o **Example**: **Amazon's Alexa** or **Google Assistant** are chatbots that use NLP to interact with users, answer questions, control devices, and perform tasks like setting reminders or playing music.

2. **Translation Apps**: Machine translation tools like **Google Translate**, **DeepL**, and **Microsoft Translator** use NLP to translate text from one language to another. These tools employ advanced algorithms, including neural machine translation (NMT), to produce more accurate and natural-sounding translations by considering the context of entire sentences rather than just translating word-by-word.

o **How NLP is used**:

- **Word Segmentation**: NLP helps segment words in languages that don't have clear spaces between words (e.g., Chinese or Japanese).

- **Contextual Understanding**: NLP models can analyze entire sentences or paragraphs, rather than individual words, to ensure that the translation maintains the proper meaning and tone.

- **Grammar and Syntax Adjustments**: NLP algorithms adjust word order and grammar to fit the rules of the target language.

o **Example**: In **Google Translate**, if you input "I am going to the store" in English, it would translate the sentence to "Voy a la tienda" in Spanish, correctly adjusting for the grammar and word order in the target language.

o **Real-Time Translation**: Modern translation apps allow for real-time conversations between speakers of different languages, such as **Skype Translator** and **iTranslate**, enabling communication between people who don't speak the same language.

---

In this chapter, we explored **Natural Language Processing (NLP)**, a vital AI discipline that focuses on enabling computers to understand and generate human language. We discussed key tasks in NLP, including **text classification**, **sentiment analysis**, and **language translation**, all of which allow machines to process and interact with text data. We also examined two real-world applications: **chatbots**, which use NLP to understand and respond to user input in conversational formats, and **translation apps**, which use NLP to translate text and speech between languages. NLP is a powerful tool in AI that has revolutionized the way we interact with technology, and its applications continue to grow in fields like customer service, content recommendation, and cross-lingual communication.

# CHAPTER 13: COMPUTER VISION: TEACHING AI TO SEE

*How Computer Vision Works*

**Computer vision** is a field of artificial intelligence that enables machines to interpret and understand visual information from the world, such as images and videos. The goal of computer vision is to allow computers to process and analyze visual data in ways similar to how humans do—identifying objects, recognizing patterns, and making sense of the environment.

Computer vision works by transforming raw image data into actionable information. This process involves several key steps:

1. **Image Acquisition**: The first step in computer vision is capturing an image or video from a camera, sensor, or other imaging device. The image is typically represented as a matrix of pixel values, where each pixel holds color or brightness information.

2. **Preprocessing**: Before processing the image, some initial steps might be taken to enhance the quality or make the image more suitable for analysis. This could include resizing, cropping, converting to grayscale (if color isn't important), noise reduction, or edge detection.

3. **Feature Extraction**: After preprocessing, the computer vision model extracts features or patterns from the image. These features could be edges, corners, textures, shapes, or more abstract concepts like regions of interest. Traditional computer vision techniques used to rely heavily on hand-crafted features, but with deep learning, the model

automatically learns relevant features from the data during training.

4. **Object Detection and Recognition**: One of the primary goals of computer vision is to identify objects within an image. This involves detecting the presence and location of objects in the image (using bounding boxes) and classifying them. Object detection models use algorithms to find objects and label them based on learned features (e.g., cat, dog, car, etc.).

5. **Classification**: Once features are extracted and objects are detected, classification models assign labels to these objects based on what they've learned from training data. For example, a model might identify an object as a "dog" or "cat" based on visual patterns it has seen during training.

6. **Post-Processing**: The final step involves refining the model's output to provide the most useful information. This could involve smoothing the results, removing false positives, or integrating predictions with other data sources for more comprehensive analysis.

Computer vision often utilizes deep learning techniques, particularly **convolutional neural networks (CNNs)**, which are designed to automatically learn the spatial hierarchies of images and efficiently process visual data.

*AI Recognizing Images and Objects*

One of the most important tasks in computer vision is **image recognition**, where an AI system identifies and classifies objects or scenes within an image. Deep learning models, particularly CNNs, have revolutionized image recognition by automatically learning to extract hierarchical features from images at multiple levels, from simple edges to complex objects.

1. **Convolutional Neural Networks (CNNs)**: CNNs are specialized neural networks designed to process image data. They are composed of several types of layers, including:
   - **Convolutional layers**: These layers apply filters (kernels) to images to extract features like edges or textures.
   - **Pooling layers**: These reduce the spatial dimensions of the image to make the representation more compact and reduce computational complexity.
   - **Fully connected layers**: These layers are responsible for classifying the image based on the features extracted by the convolutional and pooling layers.

CNNs are particularly effective at identifying spatial relationships in images, making them ideal for tasks like object detection, facial recognition, and medical image analysis.

2. **Image Classification**: Image classification is the task of assigning a label to an image based on its content. For example, in a dataset of animals, a computer vision model might classify an image as either a "cat" or "dog" based on the features it has learned.

   o **Example**: A CNN trained on images of various animals might be able to recognize an image of a dog and classify it correctly as "dog" based on learned features like fur texture, body shape, and facial structure.

3. **Object Detection**: Object detection is more complex than simple image classification because it involves locating and identifying multiple objects within an image. Object detection models, such as **YOLO (You Only Look Once)** or **Faster R-CNN**, not only classify objects but also draw bounding boxes around them to indicate their position.

   o **Example**: In an image of a busy street, object detection can identify cars, pedestrians, traffic lights, and bicycles, while also determining their locations within the image.

4. **Semantic Segmentation**: Another task within computer vision is **semantic segmentation**, which involves classifying each pixel in an image into a predefined category. Unlike object detection, which identifies entire

objects, semantic segmentation assigns a label to each pixel in the image.

- o **Example**: In an image of a park, semantic segmentation would label each pixel as either part of the sky, tree, grass, or other objects.

---

*Real-World Example: AI in Medical Imaging for Detecting Diseases*

One of the most impactful applications of computer vision is in the field of **medical imaging**, where AI is used to assist doctors in diagnosing diseases from medical images such as X-rays, MRIs, CT scans, and ultrasounds. Deep learning models, particularly CNNs, have demonstrated remarkable ability to detect patterns in medical images that might be missed by human eyes.

Here's how AI is applied in medical imaging:

1. **Image Preprocessing**: Medical images often require preprocessing to improve clarity and ensure they are in the right format for analysis. This can involve removing noise, enhancing contrast, normalizing image sizes, or adjusting brightness levels.
   - o **Example**: In CT scans or MRI images, noise reduction techniques may be applied to ensure that

the image is clear and free from artifacts that could affect diagnosis.

2. **Disease Detection**: AI models are trained to detect specific diseases or conditions from medical images. For example, a CNN might be trained to identify signs of **cancer**, **pneumonia**, **diabetic retinopathy**, or **stroke** from X-ray or MRI images. These models are trained on large datasets of labeled medical images, where the disease (or lack thereof) is marked by medical professionals.

   o **Example**: In breast cancer detection, AI models analyze mammograms to spot early signs of tumors. The AI can highlight potential areas of concern and assist radiologists in making faster, more accurate diagnoses.

3. **Image Classification and Localization**: AI systems can classify images into categories (e.g., healthy vs. diseased) or localize specific regions of interest within an image. For instance, in the case of lung disease, an AI model might identify and mark areas in an X-ray that indicate abnormalities like tumors or infections.

   o **Example**: AI models trained on lung X-rays can identify early signs of **pneumonia** or **tuberculosis** by detecting unusual patterns or opacity in the lung tissues. The model would not only classify the image as "infected" or "healthy" but also highlight the area affected by the disease.

4. **Real-Time Diagnosis and Assistance**: AI systems are used in real-time diagnostic tools, where they help medical professionals interpret images quickly. For example, AI-assisted diagnostic tools in hospitals help radiologists examine X-rays, CT scans, or MRIs more efficiently, often providing a second opinion to reduce human error.

   o **Example**: **DeepMind's AI for eye disease detection**: In a partnership with the UK's Moorfields Eye Hospital, DeepMind developed an AI system that can detect **diabetic retinopathy** and **age-related macular degeneration** from retinal scans with a level of accuracy comparable to that of expert ophthalmologists.

5. **Early Detection and Preventative Care**: AI's ability to detect diseases at an early stage is one of its most powerful applications in healthcare. Early diagnosis can significantly improve the prognosis of patients, especially in conditions like **cancer**, where early-stage detection can lead to higher survival rates.

   o **Example**: AI systems that analyze skin lesions to detect **melanoma** can identify dangerous signs of skin cancer from images taken with a simple smartphone camera, enabling early intervention and treatment.

In this chapter, we explored **computer vision**, the field of AI that enables machines to interpret and understand visual data. We discussed how computer vision models process images, recognize objects, and identify features using techniques like **convolutional neural networks (CNNs)**. We also looked at a real-world application of computer vision in **medical imaging**, where AI is used to detect diseases such as cancer, pneumonia, and diabetic retinopathy from images like X-rays and MRIs. The ability of AI to detect subtle patterns in medical images is revolutionizing healthcare, making diagnostics faster, more accurate, and available to more people. Computer vision continues to advance rapidly, with implications for a wide range of industries from healthcare to autonomous vehicles.

# CHAPTER 14: AI IN ROBOTICS: BUILDING INTELLIGENT MACHINES

*How AI is Used in Robotics*

AI plays a crucial role in modern robotics by enabling robots to perform complex tasks autonomously. Unlike traditional robots that follow pre-programmed instructions, AI-powered robots can make decisions, learn from their environment, adapt to changes, and improve over time. The integration of AI into robotics allows robots to not only follow explicit commands but also interact intelligently with their surroundings, perform tasks in dynamic environments, and handle unexpected situations.

Here are the primary ways AI is used in robotics:

1. **Perception**: Robots use **sensors** (such as cameras, LiDAR, and touch sensors) to perceive their environment. AI processes data from these sensors to interpret the world around the robot. This perception capability is essential for tasks like object detection, navigation, and interaction with people or objects.

   o **Example**: In autonomous vehicles, sensors capture the environment (roads, pedestrians, other cars), and

AI uses this data to understand the context, such as identifying obstacles or calculating the best path.

2. **Motion Planning**: AI helps robots plan and execute movements to complete tasks. Motion planning algorithms enable robots to determine how to move through space, avoid obstacles, and perform precise actions like picking up objects or navigating a maze.

   o **Example**: In industrial automation, robots equipped with AI can plan efficient routes to move items from one location to another without colliding with other objects or people.

3. **Learning and Adaptation**: AI-powered robots can use **machine learning** to improve their performance over time. By training on data or interacting with their environment, these robots can refine their abilities and adapt to new challenges without human intervention.

   o **Example**: A robot vacuum learns the layout of a room and adjusts its cleaning route for optimal efficiency, improving its cleaning patterns as it continues to operate.

4. **Decision Making**: AI enables robots to make decisions based on data input and objectives. Using algorithms such as **reinforcement learning**, robots can optimize their actions to achieve specific goals, whether it's navigating a

room, assembling a product, or providing assistance to humans.

- o **Example**: In a warehouse, a robot might decide which path to take to avoid obstacles, considering the shortest route and the potential for collisions with other robots or workers.

5. **Human-Robot Interaction (HRI)**: AI-powered robots are designed to understand human commands, gestures, or emotions, allowing for smoother collaboration between robots and humans. Through NLP (Natural Language Processing) and computer vision, robots can interpret and respond to human instructions.

- o **Example**: A social robot might use NLP to understand and respond to spoken commands, or a healthcare robot might assist elderly patients by recognizing their needs and responding appropriately.

---

### *AI-Powered Robots for Industrial Automation, Healthcare, and More*

AI-powered robots are transforming a wide range of industries by automating tasks that were previously manual, improving efficiency, accuracy, and safety. Some of the key applications include:

1. **Industrial Automation**: In manufacturing and warehouses, robots are used for tasks such as assembly, packing, sorting, and material handling. AI enables these robots to work in dynamic environments alongside humans, adapting to changes in the workflow and improving productivity.

   o **Example**: In car manufacturing, robots use AI to perform precise assembly tasks, like welding or painting, while ensuring consistency and speed. AI-driven robots in warehouses, like those used by Amazon, navigate aisles, identify products, and move them to different locations for packaging or shipping.

2. **Healthcare**: In healthcare, AI-powered robots are being used for surgery, patient care, and diagnostics. These robots assist doctors by performing repetitive tasks, assisting in delicate surgeries with high precision, and providing therapeutic interventions.

   o **Example**: **Surgical robots** like the **da Vinci Surgical System** allow surgeons to perform minimally invasive surgeries with greater precision. AI aids the system by analyzing patient data, providing insights during surgery, and improving recovery times.

o **Healthcare robots** such as **ROBOT-ASSISTED CARE**, help elderly patients with mobility issues by providing support and even monitoring vital signs.

3. **Service Industry**: AI-driven robots are increasingly used in the service industry for tasks like cleaning, food delivery, and customer interaction. These robots use AI to navigate public spaces, interact with customers, and perform tasks autonomously.

    o **Example**: AI-powered robots like **Pepper** are used in retail and hospitality settings to greet customers, provide information, and enhance the customer experience. These robots can recognize emotions and adapt their responses accordingly.

4. **Exploration and Hazardous Environments**: Robots are also deployed in environments where human presence is dangerous or impractical, such as in space exploration, underwater research, or disaster zones. AI helps these robots navigate and perform tasks in challenging conditions, where precise decision-making is critical.

    o **Example**: The **Curiosity Rover** on Mars uses AI to navigate the Martian surface and conduct scientific experiments. It processes environmental data and autonomously decides where to go and which tasks to perform next.

*Example: Robotic Vacuum Cleaners*

A well-known and widely used application of AI in robotics is the **robotic vacuum cleaner**. These autonomous devices use AI to perform cleaning tasks in homes or offices, learning the layout of a room and adjusting their cleaning paths to optimize efficiency. Let's break down how AI enables these robots to work:

1. **Perception**: Robotic vacuum cleaners are equipped with various sensors, such as infrared sensors, LiDAR, and cameras, to map their environment and detect obstacles. AI processes this sensor data to create a detailed map of the area, helping the robot navigate around furniture, walls, and other objects.

   o **Example**: A robotic vacuum cleaner like the **Roomba** uses its sensors to detect objects and navigate around furniture. If it encounters an obstacle, it adjusts its path or turns around to continue cleaning.

2. **Mapping and Navigation**: AI algorithms, particularly **Simultaneous Localization and Mapping (SLAM)**, are used by robotic vacuums to map and navigate through the cleaning area. SLAM allows the robot to create a real-time map of its environment while keeping track of its position.

   o **Example**: The robot vacuums the entire floor area by creating a map of the layout as it moves around.

Once it completes one section, it moves to the next, ensuring full coverage of the room.

3. **Learning and Adaptation**: Over time, robotic vacuum cleaners improve their performance through **machine learning**. As the robot continues to operate in the same environment, it learns the layout of the space and can plan its cleaning paths more efficiently.

   o **Example**: A robot vacuum may learn that a particular corner of the room requires extra attention or that certain obstacles (like rugs) slow it down, prompting it to alter its cleaning strategy.

4. **Task Completion**: Once the vacuum completes its cleaning task, it may autonomously return to its charging station to recharge. If the battery is low, the robot identifies the nearest charging point and navigates to it.

   o **Example**: After finishing a cleaning session, a robotic vacuum will automatically return to its docking station to charge. In some models, it can even continue cleaning once fully charged if it hasn't completed the entire area.

5. **Human-Robot Interaction**: Modern robotic vacuums often include voice control and smartphone apps that allow users to schedule cleaning sessions, monitor the robot's progress, and customize settings. These interfaces are

powered by AI and enable intuitive human-robot interaction.

- o **Example**: Users can start a cleaning cycle through voice commands via Amazon Alexa or Google Assistant, or through an app that allows users to specify areas of focus, such as cleaning specific rooms.

---

In this chapter, we explored the integration of **AI in robotics**, which enables robots to perform a wide range of tasks autonomously and intelligently. AI helps robots perceive their environment, plan their movements, make decisions, and learn from experience. We looked at how AI is applied in **industrial automation**, **healthcare**, **service industries**, and **hazardous environments** to improve efficiency, precision, and safety. A popular real-world example is the **robotic vacuum cleaner**, which uses AI to navigate, clean, and adapt to its environment. AI-powered robots are transforming industries by automating tasks, learning from their surroundings, and improving performance over time.

# CHAPTER 15: ETHICAL CONSIDERATIONS IN AI

---

## *Key Ethical Issues in AI*

The rapid development and deployment of artificial intelligence have raised numerous ethical concerns that require careful consideration. As AI systems increasingly impact our lives, from healthcare to hiring to criminal justice, the need for ethical frameworks becomes more pressing. The central ethical issues in AI revolve around how AI systems are designed, how they make decisions, and the implications of those decisions on individuals and society.

Some of the key ethical issues in AI include:

1. **Bias and Fairness**: AI systems are often criticized for perpetuating or even exacerbating biases present in the data they are trained on. If an AI model is trained on biased data—whether in terms of gender, race, age, or other factors—it can produce biased outputs that reinforce existing inequalities. The challenge is ensuring that AI systems are fair and do not discriminate against marginalized groups.

2. **Accountability**: When AI systems make decisions that affect individuals, such as loan approvals, hiring decisions, or legal sentencing, it's important to determine who is responsible when something goes wrong. The lack of transparency and explainability in many AI systems can make it difficult to assign accountability for their actions.

3. **Privacy**: AI systems often require large amounts of data to function, which raises concerns about privacy. How is personal data collected, used, and protected? Who owns the data, and how do we ensure that individuals have control over their own information?

4. **Autonomy and Control**: As AI systems become more autonomous, there are concerns about whether humans will retain control over important decision-making processes. This is particularly concerning in high-stakes domains like autonomous weapons or self-driving cars, where AI could make life-or-death decisions without human oversight.

5. **Transparency and Explainability**: Many AI models, especially deep learning models, operate as "black boxes," meaning their decision-making processes are not easily understood. This lack of transparency raises concerns about whether these systems can be trusted to make decisions that align with human values and ethical standards.

6. **Job Displacement**: As AI systems automate more tasks, there are concerns about job displacement. While AI and automation have the potential to increase productivity, they also risk leaving certain workers without employment, particularly in industries that rely on routine or manual labor.

---

### *Bias, Fairness, and Accountability in AI Systems*

AI systems can inherit and even amplify biases from the data they are trained on, leading to unfair or discriminatory outcomes. Addressing these issues is crucial to ensuring that AI systems are ethical, equitable, and accountable.

1. **Bias in AI**: Bias in AI occurs when an AI system reflects or amplifies prejudices present in the data it was trained on. These biases can arise from many sources, such as historical inequalities in the data, unrepresentative training samples, or biased human decisions that influence the data.

- o **Example**: If a hiring algorithm is trained on historical data from a company that has predominantly hired men for engineering roles, the algorithm may learn to favor male candidates, perpetuating gender inequality in hiring.

2. **Fairness**: Fairness in AI refers to the idea that AI systems should treat all individuals equally and impartially, without discriminating based on characteristics such as race, gender, or age. Ensuring fairness requires identifying and addressing biases in training data and developing models that are less sensitive to irrelevant variables.

   - o **Example**: In criminal justice, AI systems that predict recidivism (the likelihood of a criminal reoffending) have been criticized for unfairly targeting minority groups due to biases in the data. These systems might disproportionately classify African American defendants as high risk based on biased historical data, even though race is not a legitimate factor in determining risk.

3. **Accountability**: Accountability in AI systems refers to the need for clear responsibility when an AI system makes decisions that impact people's lives. If an AI system causes harm, whether it's an unjust hiring decision or an unfair legal outcome, we need to ensure that there is a mechanism

to hold the developers, organizations, or entities using the AI accountable.

- o **Example**: If a self-driving car makes a mistake and causes an accident, who is responsible? The manufacturer? The software developer? The owner of the car? Accountability is complex in AI systems, especially when the decision-making process is opaque or when the system is largely autonomous.

---

*Example: Bias in Hiring Algorithms*

One of the most discussed ethical issues in AI is the use of algorithms in hiring and recruitment processes. While AI can make hiring more efficient and objective by screening resumes or analyzing job candidates' data, these systems can also reinforce existing biases in the workforce if not carefully monitored.

1. **How Hiring Algorithms Work**: Many companies use AI-powered hiring tools to scan resumes, conduct initial screening interviews, or even rank job candidates based on their qualifications, skills, and other factors. These algorithms are often trained on historical hiring data, which includes past decisions made by recruiters or companies.

2. **The Problem of Bias**: If the historical data used to train the hiring algorithm reflects existing biases—such as favoring

male candidates for technical positions or overlooking candidates from certain ethnic backgrounds—the AI model will learn these patterns and reproduce them in its recommendations. This can perpetuate gender, racial, or other forms of discrimination in hiring.

- o **Example**: Amazon's AI recruitment tool, which was intended to help automate the hiring process, was found to be biased against female candidates. The system was trained on resumes submitted to Amazon over a 10-year period, which were predominantly from male candidates, leading the algorithm to favor male-dominated job profiles and inadvertently penalize resumes with female-associated words like "women's" or "female."

3. **Ensuring Fairness**: To mitigate bias in hiring algorithms, companies must take several steps:

- o **Diversifying Training Data**: Ensure that the training data used to build AI models is diverse and representative of the candidates the system will encounter in real life. For instance, historical hiring data should be carefully analyzed to remove any gender, racial, or other biases.

- o **Bias Detection and Testing**: Regularly test AI systems for bias by analyzing their decisions and outcomes. If an algorithm is found to be biased, adjustments should be made to correct it.

o **Transparency and Explainability**: AI models should be explainable, meaning that employers and candidates can understand how the system arrived at a particular decision. This can help avoid "black-box" systems that make it difficult to identify or address bias.

o **Human Oversight**: While AI can assist in the hiring process, human oversight is critical. Final hiring decisions should always involve a human review to ensure fairness and to provide accountability for the decisions made by the AI system.

---

In this chapter, we explored **ethical considerations in AI**, focusing on key issues like **bias, fairness**, and **accountability**. AI systems, while powerful, can inherit and even amplify biases from the data they are trained on, leading to discriminatory outcomes. We discussed how **bias in hiring algorithms** is a common example of this issue, where AI systems can unintentionally perpetuate gender, racial, or other forms of discrimination. To address these concerns, AI systems must be designed with fairness in mind, regularly tested for bias, and made transparent and accountable. Ethical AI development is essential to ensuring that

AI systems are used responsibly, promoting equity and trust in their deployment across industries.

# CHAPTER 16: AI AND THE JOB MARKET: OPPORTUNITIES AND CHALLENGES

*How AI is Transforming Jobs and Industries*

AI is rapidly transforming the job market, reshaping industries, and altering the way work is performed. While it offers significant opportunities to increase efficiency, productivity, and innovation, AI also presents challenges related to workforce displacement, job transformation, and the need for new skills.

1. **Automation of Routine Tasks**: AI and automation technologies are particularly effective at performing repetitive, rule-based tasks, which are common in industries like manufacturing, retail, and customer service. By automating these tasks, businesses can streamline operations and reduce costs, but this also leads to job displacement, particularly for low-skill, manual jobs.

   o **Example**: In the manufacturing sector, AI-driven robots can assemble products, weld parts, or perform quality control checks. In customer service, AI chatbots can handle routine inquiries, such as checking account balances or answering FAQs.

2. **Enhancing Human Capabilities**: Rather than replacing humans entirely, AI is also used to augment human capabilities. In many industries, AI tools assist workers in making better decisions, optimizing workflows, and improving productivity. This allows employees to focus on higher-level tasks that require creativity, problem-solving, and interpersonal skills.

   o **Example**: In healthcare, AI tools assist doctors by analyzing medical images, suggesting potential diagnoses, and helping with treatment planning. This doesn't replace doctors but allows them to make more informed decisions more quickly.

3. **Creating New Jobs and Industries**: While AI will undoubtedly displace some jobs, it also creates new opportunities. AI will drive the demand for new types of jobs in fields such as data science, machine learning engineering, and AI ethics. Additionally, as businesses adopt AI, there will be a growing need for roles focused on managing AI systems, developing new applications, and ensuring their responsible use.

   o **Example**: The rise of autonomous vehicles has created new job opportunities in autonomous systems engineering, vehicle maintenance for AI-powered fleets, and safety protocol development.

4. **Job Transformation**: Many jobs will evolve due to AI. For example, a traditional administrative assistant's role may be augmented by AI tools for scheduling, email management, and document processing, allowing the worker to focus on tasks that require more creativity or human interaction. AI will enable workers to take on more strategic roles while handling routine aspects of the job.

   o **Example**: In finance, AI-driven algorithms can automate trading and market analysis, but financial analysts will still be required to interpret AI findings and make strategic investment decisions.

*The Future of Work in an AI-Driven World*

The future of work will be significantly influenced by AI, but the exact nature of this transformation remains uncertain. While AI presents opportunities for innovation and increased productivity, it also presents challenges related to inequality, job displacement, and ethical considerations.

1. **AI and Workforce Displacement**: A key concern about AI is its potential to displace jobs, particularly in sectors where automation can replace human labor. Many routine jobs, especially those involving repetitive tasks, are at risk. According to reports by organizations like the **World Economic Forum**, millions of jobs will be displaced by AI and automation over the next few decades.

   o **Example**: In retail, cashier positions may be replaced by self-checkout systems or AI-powered inventory management tools. Similarly, many customer service roles are being automated through chatbots and virtual assistants.

2. **AI and Skill Gaps**: The widespread adoption of AI will require workers to acquire new skills, particularly in technology, data analysis, and AI system management. There will be an increasing demand for workers who are skilled in programming, machine learning, and AI ethics. However, the gap between the skills workers have and the

skills they need is a major challenge, particularly for workers in sectors that are most at risk of automation.

- o **Example**: A worker in a factory that previously assembled products may need to retrain to operate and maintain automated machines or focus on higher-level tasks such as managing the production process.

3. **AI and Job Creation**: While AI will automate many jobs, it will also create new roles that don't exist today. These include positions focused on AI development, AI model training, human-AI collaboration, and AI regulation. The challenge will be ensuring that displaced workers have access to reskilling programs and are able to transition to these new roles.

- o **Example**: In the tech sector, there will be an increased demand for machine learning engineers, data scientists, and AI ethicists who can ensure that AI systems are developed and used responsibly.

4. **Human-AI Collaboration**: The future of work in an AI-driven world will likely involve more human-AI collaboration. AI will handle the repetitive and data-heavy tasks, while humans will focus on creative, strategic, and emotional tasks that require judgment, empathy, and flexibility.

o **Example**: In healthcare, AI might assist doctors in diagnosing diseases by analyzing medical images, but doctors will remain responsible for patient interactions, providing empathy, and making complex treatment decisions.

---

## *Real-World Example: AI in Customer Service Automation*

One of the most prominent examples of AI's impact on the job market is its role in **customer service automation**. AI is transforming the way companies interact with customers, particularly in industries like retail, banking, and telecommunications.

Here's how AI is used in customer service:

1. **AI Chatbots and Virtual Assistants**: AI chatbots are commonly used to handle customer inquiries, providing instant responses to routine questions or directing customers to the appropriate resources. These chatbots use natural language processing (NLP) to understand and respond to text or voice input. They can answer questions, provide product recommendations, and even process transactions.

   o **Example**: **Banking chatbots**, like those used by Bank of America (Erica) or Capital One (Eno), can assist customers with tasks like checking account balances, transferring funds, or providing information about credit card transactions—all without human intervention.

2. **Automated Phone Systems**: AI-driven voice assistants are increasingly used to manage customer service calls, enabling businesses to automate interactions with customers over the phone. These systems can understand spoken language and carry out tasks like processing orders, handling complaints, or scheduling appointments.

   o **Example**: **Amazon Alexa** or **Google Assistant** is used by companies to automate phone-based customer service, providing instant responses to basic inquiries or guiding customers through troubleshooting steps.

3. **Sentiment Analysis**: AI is also used to analyze customer interactions for sentiment, allowing companies to understand how customers feel about their products or services. By analyzing tone, word choice, and context in customer emails, social media posts, or phone calls, AI models can detect frustration or satisfaction and help businesses respond more effectively.

   o **Example**: **Zendesk's AI tools** analyze customer support tickets and provide recommendations to support agents about how to respond based on sentiment analysis, helping agents focus on the most urgent or sensitive issues.

4. **AI-Powered Help Desks**: Many companies now use AI to power their help desk systems, which can quickly resolve common customer issues or escalate more complex problems to human agents. AI tools can automate ticket routing, categorize issues, and even suggest solutions based on historical data.

   o **Example: Freshdesk** uses AI to automate repetitive tasks like ticket categorization and prioritization, helping customer support teams respond more quickly and efficiently.

---

In this chapter, we explored how **AI is transforming jobs and industries** by automating routine tasks, enhancing human capabilities, and creating new roles. While AI promises significant productivity gains, it also presents challenges, including job displacement and the need for reskilling. The future of work will require a balance between automation and human involvement, with opportunities for new types of jobs that didn't exist before. We also discussed a real-world example of **AI in customer service automation**, where chatbots, virtual assistants, and sentiment analysis tools are changing the way businesses interact with customers. AI's role in customer service is just one example of how it's reshaping industries, making work more efficient, and creating new opportunities and challenges in the job market.

# CHAPTER 17: AI IN EVERYDAY LIFE: PRACTICAL APPLICATIONS

### *AI Applications in Daily Life*

AI has become an integral part of our daily lives, often working behind the scenes to enhance convenience, efficiency, and personalization. From smartphones and home devices to financial management and shopping, AI is transforming how we interact with technology and how technology interacts with us.

In this chapter, we'll explore the diverse and practical applications of AI that we encounter in our daily routines. These AI applications improve our productivity, save time, and offer a more personalized experience.

---

### 1. AI in Smartphones

Smartphones are among the most common devices that incorporate AI to enhance user experience. AI in smartphones is utilized for a variety of tasks, from voice assistants to photo enhancement and personalized recommendations.

1. **Virtual Assistants**: AI-powered virtual assistants like **Apple's Siri**, **Google Assistant**, and **Amazon's Alexa** are integrated into smartphones to perform tasks such as setting reminders, making calls, sending texts, providing weather updates, and answering questions. These assistants use natural language processing (NLP) and machine learning to understand spoken language and respond intelligently.

   o **Example**: With Siri, you can ask, "What's the weather like today?" and Siri will analyze your query using NLP and return the correct weather forecast.

2. **Personalized Recommendations**: AI learns from your behavior and usage patterns on your phone to provide recommendations. This can include suggesting apps, music, or videos based on your interests and activities. For instance, **YouTube** and **Spotify** use AI to recommend videos or playlists based on your previous consumption habits.

   o **Example**: Spotify uses AI to curate daily playlists like **Discover Weekly**, tailoring music suggestions based on your listening history.

3. **Smart Photography**: AI is also used in smartphones for camera enhancements. Through **AI-powered image recognition**, phones can automatically adjust settings such as lighting, contrast, and focus to capture the best possible photos.

   o **Example**: The **Google Pixel** phone uses AI in its camera to improve image quality, particularly in low-light conditions, and can even recognize objects, scenes, and faces, automatically optimizing photos for the best results.

4. **Battery Optimization**: AI in smartphones can optimize battery life by learning how you use your phone and adjusting settings like background app activity or brightness.

○ **Example**: AI-driven **battery management** in smartphones can learn your charging habits and intelligently manage power distribution to maximize battery longevity.

---

## 2. AI in Home Devices

AI is increasingly embedded in **smart home devices**, providing homeowners with more control, convenience, and automation in their daily lives. From voice-controlled assistants to intelligent thermostats, AI plays a key role in home automation.

1. **Smart Home Assistants**: Devices like **Amazon Echo** and **Google Nest Hub** allow users to control various aspects of their home environment through voice commands. These devices use NLP to understand and execute commands such as controlling lights, adjusting temperature, or playing music.

   ○ **Example**: **Amazon Echo** (powered by Alexa) can control smart home devices, like turning lights on/off, adjusting your thermostat, or locking doors, all through voice commands. You can say, "Alexa, turn off the living room lights," and the device will automatically perform the action.

2. **Smart Thermostats**: AI-powered thermostats like **Nest** and **Ecobee** learn your heating and cooling preferences over time and adjust your home's temperature accordingly. These devices use **machine learning** to optimize energy consumption, making homes more energy-efficient.

   o **Example**: **Nest Thermostat** learns your schedule and temperature preferences, adjusting the climate in your home automatically. It can also save energy by learning when you're away and adjusting the temperature to reduce heating or cooling costs.

3. **Smart Security Systems**: AI plays a significant role in **smart security systems**, such as **Ring** and **Nest Cam**, which use **computer vision** and AI to identify people, monitor activity, and even send alerts to homeowners when unusual movements are detected.

   o **Example**: **Ring Video Doorbell** uses AI to detect motion, recognize familiar faces, and alert homeowners when someone is at the door. It can differentiate between people, animals, and inanimate objects, reducing false alarms.

---

### *3. AI in Personal Finance Apps*

AI has made a significant impact on personal finance, with applications designed to help individuals manage their money more effectively. AI-powered finance apps can track spending, automate savings, and offer personalized financial advice.

1. **Expense Tracking**: AI-driven apps like **Mint** or **YNAB (You Need a Budget)** analyze your spending patterns and categorize expenses automatically. This helps users gain insights into where their money is going, identify areas to cut back, and stay on track with their financial goals.

   o **Example**: **Mint** categorizes your purchases (e.g., groceries, entertainment, utilities) and provides an overview of your spending habits, helping you stay within budget.

2. **Automated Saving and Investing**: AI-powered tools like **Acorns** and **Betterment** automate the process of saving and investing. These platforms analyze your financial habits and automatically round up purchases to the nearest dollar, investing the change, or suggest personalized investment portfolios based on your goals and risk tolerance.

   o **Example**: **Acorns** automatically invests spare change from everyday purchases into diversified portfolios. For instance, if you buy a coffee for $2.75, Acorns rounds up the purchase to $3.00 and invests the $0.25 difference.

3. **Personalized Financial Advice**: Robo-advisors use AI to provide automated, personalized financial advice. These

platforms analyze users' financial situations, risk preferences, and goals, offering tailored investment strategies without the need for human advisors.

- o **Example**: **Betterment** is an AI-driven robo-advisor that creates customized investment plans based on your financial goals, such as retirement or buying a house. It automatically rebalances your portfolio and adjusts your strategy based on market conditions.

---

### 4. AI in E-Commerce Recommendations

AI is also transforming e-commerce by personalizing the shopping experience for users, making it easier for customers to find products they are likely to purchase.

1. **Product Recommendations**: AI algorithms analyze customers' browsing behavior, past purchases, and preferences to recommend products they are most likely to buy. These recommendations are often displayed as "you may also like" suggestions on product pages or in personalized email campaigns.

   - o **Example**: **Amazon** uses AI to recommend products based on your previous searches and purchases. If you buy a set of headphones, Amazon may suggest related items such as Bluetooth speakers, carrying cases, or other electronics.

2. **Personalized Pricing**: AI in e-commerce can also be used for dynamic pricing, where the cost of products can fluctuate based on demand, competitor pricing, and user behavior. This allows retailers to adjust prices to maximize profits or offer personalized discounts.

   o **Example**: **Uber** uses dynamic pricing algorithms to adjust fares based on supply and demand. During peak hours or bad weather, Uber's AI may increase the price of rides to match demand.

3. **Chatbots for Customer Service**: Many e-commerce platforms use AI-powered chatbots to assist customers in real-time. These bots can help users track orders, answer product questions, or even guide them through the purchasing process.

   o **Example**: **Sephora's chatbot** helps customers find the perfect beauty products based on their preferences. It can recommend makeup shades based on skin tone or offer personalized skincare routines.

In this chapter, we examined the wide-ranging **practical applications of AI** in everyday life, from **smartphones** and **home devices** to **personal finance apps** and **e-commerce**

**recommendations**. AI is revolutionizing how we interact with technology, making our lives more efficient, personalized, and convenient. AI-powered **virtual assistants** and **smart home devices** automate tasks and provide personalized experiences, while AI in **personal finance** helps individuals manage their money more effectively. In the world of **e-commerce**, AI enhances the shopping experience by recommending products and offering personalized pricing. As AI continues to evolve, we can expect even more innovative applications that make daily tasks easier and more intuitive.

# CHAPTER 18: AI AND HEALTHCARE: REVOLUTIONIZING MEDICINE

### *AI Applications in Healthcare*

AI is transforming healthcare by improving efficiency, accuracy, and accessibility in both clinical settings and medical research. From diagnosing diseases to discovering new drugs, AI is helping medical professionals provide better care, reduce human error, and speed up the development of treatments.

AI in healthcare can be broadly categorized into the following applications:

1. **Diagnosis and Disease Detection**: AI systems can assist doctors by analyzing medical data, such as images, lab results, and patient history, to identify diseases and conditions more accurately and quickly than traditional methods.

2. **Drug Discovery and Development**: AI accelerates the process of discovering new drugs by predicting how different compounds will interact with the body. This significantly shortens the timeline for developing new medications, which traditionally takes many years.

3. **Personalized Medicine**: AI can help tailor treatments to individual patients by analyzing genetic information,

medical history, and lifestyle data to create personalized treatment plans. This approach leads to better outcomes and minimizes side effects.

4. **Medical Imaging**: AI is revolutionizing medical imaging by helping radiologists and clinicians interpret images such as X-rays, MRIs, and CT scans with greater precision. AI can identify subtle patterns that might be missed by the human eye.

5. **Virtual Health Assistants**: AI-powered virtual assistants are becoming more common in healthcare, helping patients manage their health by providing reminders for medication, answering health-related questions, and even monitoring vital signs remotely.

6. **Clinical Decision Support**: AI systems are used to analyze patient data in real-time to provide recommendations for clinical decisions. This can help doctors make more informed decisions about diagnosis and treatment plans, improving patient outcomes.

## *AI in Diagnosis, Drug Discovery, and Personalized Medicine*

1. **AI in Diagnosis and Disease Detection**: AI is increasingly being used in diagnostic tools, where it helps doctors identify conditions earlier and more accurately. By

analyzing large volumes of medical data, AI can spot patterns that indicate the presence of a disease, sometimes even before symptoms appear.

- **Medical Imaging**: AI is particularly effective in analyzing medical images. **Deep learning** algorithms, such as **convolutional neural networks (CNNs)**, are used to detect abnormalities in medical scans, including X-rays, MRIs, and CT scans.

- **Example**: In **breast cancer diagnosis**, AI-powered systems analyze mammograms to identify signs of tumors or irregular tissue. AI can detect small tumors with a high degree of accuracy, sometimes identifying issues that might be missed by human radiologists.

- **Example**: In **diabetic retinopathy**, AI is used to scan retinal images and detect early signs of damage caused by diabetes, enabling early intervention to prevent vision loss.

2. **AI in Drug Discovery**: Traditional drug discovery can take many years and cost billions of dollars. AI is transforming this process by analyzing vast datasets of molecular structures, predicting how different compounds interact with the body, and identifying potential new drugs much more quickly.

- o **Example**: **Atomwise**, an AI-powered company, uses machine learning algorithms to predict the effectiveness of various chemical compounds against specific diseases. In 2014, Atomwise's AI model helped discover a compound that could potentially treat the Ebola virus, speeding up the drug discovery process.

- o **Example**: **Insilico Medicine** uses AI to design molecules for drug candidates. By using deep learning models to simulate how molecules interact with biological targets, they can identify promising compounds that can then be tested in labs.

3. **AI in Personalized Medicine**: Personalized medicine tailors treatment plans to individual patients based on their genetic makeup, lifestyle, and other personal factors. AI helps create these personalized treatment plans by analyzing large datasets of medical records, genetic data, and lifestyle information to identify the most effective therapies.

   - o **Example**: In **cancer treatment**, AI can analyze genomic data from a patient's tumor and compare it to a database of known cancerous mutations. Based on this analysis, doctors can prescribe personalized treatment plans, including targeted therapies and immunotherapies.

o **Example**: In **pharmacogenomics**, AI is used to predict how different individuals will respond to various drugs based on their genetic profiles, ensuring that patients receive the most effective treatment with the least risk of side effects.

---

## *Real-World Example: AI in Diagnostic Tools Like X-Ray Analysis*

One of the most impactful uses of AI in healthcare is in the analysis of medical imaging, such as **X-rays**, **MRIs**, and **CT scans**. AI's ability to process and analyze images has greatly enhanced diagnostic accuracy and efficiency, particularly in areas like radiology.

1. **AI-Powered X-Ray Analysis**: AI is being used to help radiologists interpret X-ray images faster and with greater accuracy. Deep learning algorithms, particularly **convolutional neural networks (CNNs)**, are trained to recognize patterns in X-ray images that indicate the presence of disease, such as **lung cancer**, **pneumonia**, or **fractures**.

   o **Example**: **Zebra Medical Vision** developed an AI algorithm that analyzes X-rays and CT scans to detect a variety of conditions. Their AI system can identify cardiovascular problems, lung diseases, and even certain types of cancers at an early stage, allowing for earlier intervention.

- o **Example**: **Google Health** developed an AI system that can detect **breast cancer** in mammograms with greater accuracy than human radiologists. The AI system was trained on thousands of mammogram images, learning to recognize subtle signs of cancer. The result is a diagnostic tool that improves both the speed and accuracy of breast cancer detection.

2. **AI in Radiology**: AI has been a game-changer for radiologists, assisting them with the interpretation of complex imaging studies. AI-powered systems can highlight areas of concern within an image, flagging them for the attention of a radiologist, and even making preliminary diagnoses.

- o **Example**: **Aidoc**, an AI company, developed a tool that analyzes CT scans for conditions like brain hemorrhages, stroke, and spinal injuries. The AI scans the images and flags potential issues for the radiologist to review, improving the speed and accuracy of diagnoses.

3. **Real-Time Assistance**: AI can provide real-time feedback, enabling quicker decision-making and improving patient care. Radiologists and doctors no longer need to manually

review every image in detail; instead, AI can highlight areas of concern, allowing healthcare professionals to focus on critical tasks.

- o **Example: VUNO Med** is an AI-driven system that can analyze X-rays and CT scans in real-time, offering immediate results. This reduces the time it takes for doctors to review results and make treatment decisions, particularly in emergency situations.

In this chapter, we explored how **AI is revolutionizing healthcare**, with applications that span **diagnosis, drug discovery**, and **personalized medicine**. AI-powered diagnostic tools, such as those used for **X-ray analysis**, help doctors detect diseases like cancer, pneumonia, and fractures more quickly and accurately. AI is also playing a pivotal role in **drug discovery** by predicting molecular interactions and speeding up the development of new treatments. Additionally, **personalized medicine** is being transformed by AI, which tailors treatments to individual patients based on their genetic and personal data. As AI continues to advance, its role in healthcare will grow, enabling faster, more accurate diagnoses, more effective treatments, and better overall patient outcomes.

# CHAPTER 19: AI IN TRANSPORTATION: SELF-DRIVING CARS

*How AI is Transforming Transportation*

AI is having a profound impact on the transportation industry, driving innovations that promise to make travel safer, more efficient, and more accessible. From **self-driving cars** to AI-powered logistics systems, the use of AI is reshaping the way goods and people move around the world. Below are the key ways AI is transforming transportation:

1. **Autonomous Vehicles**: One of the most talked-about applications of AI in transportation is the development of **autonomous vehicles (AVs)**, or self-driving cars. These vehicles use AI, sensors, and machine learning algorithms to navigate roads without human intervention. AI-powered systems in self-driving cars can process vast amounts of data in real-time, making driving decisions such as braking, accelerating, steering, and detecting obstacles.

   o **Example**: Companies like **Waymo** (a subsidiary of Alphabet) and **Tesla** are at the forefront of developing autonomous vehicles. These vehicles use AI to understand their environment, make decisions, and navigate roads safely, with the ultimate goal of reducing human driving errors, improving safety, and increasing efficiency.

2. **AI in Traffic Management**: AI can be used to optimize traffic flow and reduce congestion. Smart traffic lights powered by AI can adjust their timings based on traffic patterns, ensuring smoother traffic movement and reducing wait times at intersections. AI can also be used in **route planning**, helping both personal vehicles and delivery trucks find the fastest, most efficient routes.

   o **Example**: **AI-powered traffic systems** in cities like **Los Angeles** and **Singapore** use real-time data to adjust traffic signals and improve the flow of traffic, reducing congestion and emissions.

3. **AI in Logistics and Fleet Management**: AI is revolutionizing logistics by improving fleet management, supply chain optimization, and predictive maintenance. AI systems can track deliveries in real-time, optimize routes for fuel efficiency, and predict when vehicles will require maintenance, reducing downtime and operational costs.

   o **Example**: Companies like **UPS** and **FedEx** are using AI to optimize delivery routes, reduce fuel consumption, and improve delivery times. AI-powered systems in these companies analyze data such as weather patterns, traffic, and parcel destinations to determine the most efficient routes for drivers.

4. **Electric and Connected Vehicles**: Many autonomous vehicles are also connected and electric. AI in connected cars enables them to communicate with each other and the surrounding infrastructure, improving safety and navigation. Autonomous electric vehicles (EVs) also benefit from AI-driven energy management systems that optimize battery use and charging schedules.

   o **Example**: **Tesla** vehicles use AI to manage everything from energy consumption to self-driving capabilities, creating a seamless and efficient driving experience.

## Self-Driving Cars and AI in Logistics

1. **Self-Driving Cars**: Self-driving cars use AI to perform a variety of functions that allow them to drive without human intervention. These vehicles rely on a combination of **computer vision**, **LIDAR** (Light Detection and Ranging), **radar**, and **machine learning** to understand and interpret the world around them. They must be able to make real-

time decisions based on this data to navigate roads, avoid obstacles, and follow traffic laws.

- **Core Technologies Behind Self-Driving Cars**:
    - **Computer Vision**: AI systems use cameras and image recognition to identify road signs, pedestrians, other vehicles, and obstacles in the car's path.
    - **LIDAR and Radar**: These sensors provide 3D maps of the environment, helping the car detect and understand its surroundings in real-time, even in low visibility conditions.
    - **Machine Learning**: AI-powered self-driving systems continually learn from their experiences. As they are exposed to more data (e.g., road conditions, driver behavior), their algorithms improve, allowing the cars to make more accurate predictions and decisions.

2. **AI in Logistics**: The same AI technologies used in self-driving cars are being applied to logistics, where they can improve fleet management and delivery operations. Autonomous trucks, for example, can navigate highways and city streets with minimal human intervention, reducing the cost of labor and increasing delivery efficiency.

- **Example**: **Waymo** is working on developing autonomous trucking solutions, using AI to optimize delivery routes and reduce human driver fatigue. AI systems in logistics companies can also analyze traffic patterns, weather forecasts, and route data to optimize deliveries and minimize delays.

- **Example**: **TuSimple** is a company specializing in autonomous trucks. Their trucks use AI to drive long distances on highways with minimal human input, saving fuel and reducing operating costs. The technology is aimed at revolutionizing the freight transport industry.

3. **AI in Delivery Drones**: AI is also being used in **drone deliveries**, where AI systems help drones navigate through urban environments, avoid obstacles, and deliver packages autonomously. AI-driven drones are seen as a potential solution to last-mile delivery, offering faster and more efficient delivery methods, especially in urban areas.

   - **Example**: **Amazon Prime Air** is testing autonomous delivery drones that use AI to navigate through the air, deliver small packages to customers' doorsteps, and avoid obstacles. AI plays a critical role in ensuring that drones can make real-time decisions about flight paths and avoid collisions.

*Real-World Example: Tesla's Autopilot System*

Tesla's **Autopilot** system is one of the most well-known applications of AI in self-driving cars. Tesla has integrated AI and machine learning technologies into its vehicles, allowing them to perform some driving tasks autonomously. While full autonomy has not yet been achieved, Tesla's Autopilot system offers a glimpse into the future of self-driving vehicles.

1. **Core Features of Tesla's Autopilot**: Tesla's Autopilot system is equipped with a variety of sensors, including cameras, radar, and ultrasonic sensors, to understand the environment around the vehicle. AI-powered computer vision helps Tesla's cars identify objects, lane markings, and traffic signals, while machine learning algorithms make real-time decisions about acceleration, braking, and steering.

    o **Example**: Tesla's Autopilot can steer the car within its lane, accelerate and decelerate in response to traffic conditions, and change lanes autonomously. The system uses real-time data to make decisions about when to apply the brakes, speed up, or slow down, depending on the surrounding environment.

2. **Tesla's Full Self-Driving (FSD) Capability**: Tesla's **Full Self-Driving (FSD)** package, which is still under

development, promises to enable vehicles to navigate fully autonomously in urban environments, including turning at intersections and handling stop signs. While the system is still being tested and refined, it showcases Tesla's ambitious goal to develop fully autonomous vehicles.

- o **Example**: With FSD, Tesla cars can navigate from highway onramps to offramps, park themselves, and even recognize stop signs and traffic lights. The car's AI system is continually updated through over-the-air software updates, making it smarter and more capable with each iteration.

3. **Continuous Learning and Improvement**: Tesla's AI system is constantly learning from the data collected by Tesla vehicles on the road. Tesla vehicles are equipped with cameras that capture data about their surroundings, which is then processed and used to improve the AI models. This creates a feedback loop where Tesla's cars get smarter over time.

- o **Example**: As more Teslas are driven with Autopilot engaged, the AI system learns from millions of miles of data. This allows Tesla to improve its algorithms, enabling better decision-making in various driving scenarios, such as complex city streets or adverse weather conditions.

4. **Human-in-the-Loop**: Although Tesla's Autopilot and FSD systems are advanced, they are not yet fully autonomous. Tesla vehicles still require the driver to pay attention and be ready to take control of the car at any time. Tesla's system includes a monitoring feature to ensure the driver's hands are on the wheel, and it can alert the driver if they're not paying attention.

   o **Example**: In situations where the AI system encounters an unexpected obstacle or complex road scenario, the driver is expected to intervene. Tesla's Autopilot is considered a driver assistance feature, rather than fully autonomous driving.

In this chapter, we explored how **AI is transforming transportation**, particularly through the development of **self-driving cars** and AI-powered logistics. AI systems enable vehicles to navigate, detect obstacles, and make real-time decisions, which can potentially reduce accidents, improve traffic flow, and enhance efficiency in freight and delivery systems. We also looked at **Tesla's Autopilot** as a real-world example of AI in self-driving cars. While Tesla's technology is still evolving, it offers a glimpse into the future of autonomous driving and showcases how AI can continually learn from real-world data to improve performance. As AI continues to advance, the transportation industry is set to undergo significant changes, with autonomous vehicles, smarter logistics, and improved efficiency shaping the future of mobility.

# CHAPTER 20: AI AND THE ENVIRONMENT: SUSTAINABLE SOLUTIONS

### *AI's Role in Addressing Environmental Challenges*

As the world faces pressing environmental challenges, AI is emerging as a powerful tool for creating sustainable solutions. From reducing energy consumption and predicting climate change to optimizing waste management systems, AI has the potential to accelerate progress in environmental conservation and improve the efficiency of resource use. By leveraging AI's ability to process vast amounts of data, recognize patterns, and make predictions, we can better understand and address environmental issues that threaten the planet's future.

Key areas where AI can contribute to environmental sustainability include:

1. **Energy Efficiency and Smart Energy Systems**: AI can optimize energy consumption, making systems more efficient by predicting demand, adjusting supply, and minimizing waste. By using AI to manage the distribution

of energy, we can reduce carbon footprints and improve the sustainability of energy systems.

2. **Climate Modeling and Prediction**: AI models can analyze large datasets from satellites, sensors, and climate records to predict climate patterns and changes. By making more accurate predictions, AI can help scientists and policymakers mitigate the effects of climate change and plan for future environmental scenarios.

3. **Waste Management**: AI can optimize waste management by improving recycling processes, identifying waste patterns, and automating sorting. AI-powered solutions can help reduce landfill waste, improve recycling rates, and create more efficient waste management systems.

4. **Biodiversity Conservation**: AI can help monitor biodiversity and track endangered species. By analyzing data from drones, cameras, and sensors, AI can help track ecosystems and support conservation efforts.

5. **Sustainable Agriculture**: AI technologies can optimize farming practices, reduce water usage, and minimize pesticide and fertilizer usage, contributing to more sustainable food production.

---

*Smart Energy Systems, Climate Modeling, and Waste Management*

1. **Smart Energy Systems**: One of the most promising applications of AI in environmental sustainability is in **smart energy systems**, particularly in the management and optimization of energy distribution. AI-powered systems can adjust energy use in real-time based on demand, weather conditions, and availability of renewable energy sources.

   o **Smart Grids**: **Smart grids** use AI to optimize electricity distribution by automatically adjusting the flow of energy depending on demand and the availability of renewable energy (such as solar or wind power). This helps prevent energy waste, balance supply and demand, and integrate renewable energy sources more efficiently.

     ▪ **Example**: In a **smart grid**, AI algorithms forecast energy demand by analyzing historical usage data, weather patterns, and consumer behavior. The system can then predict when energy demand will peak and adjust energy distribution accordingly, ensuring the most efficient use of resources. Additionally, AI can predict outages and divert power to prevent service interruptions, making the grid more resilient.

- o **Energy Consumption Optimization**: AI can also help consumers and businesses optimize their energy use by analyzing patterns and providing recommendations for energy-saving measures.
    - **Example**: Smart home systems, such as **Google Nest** or **Amazon Alexa**, use AI to learn user preferences and optimize heating, cooling, and lighting in homes, reducing energy consumption and lowering utility bills.

2. **Climate Modeling and Prediction**: AI is being increasingly used in **climate modeling** to predict environmental changes and simulate various climate scenarios. With the help of machine learning algorithms, scientists can analyze vast amounts of climate data and make more accurate predictions about the future effects of climate change.

    - o **Climate Prediction Models**: By processing satellite imagery, weather patterns, and environmental data, AI can help predict future climate conditions, such as temperature changes, precipitation patterns, and sea level rise.
        - **Example**: AI models have been used to predict the impact of **global warming** on ecosystems, biodiversity, and agricultural

productivity. For instance, AI can help model how rising temperatures will affect crop yields, allowing farmers to adjust practices and mitigate risks.

- o **Disaster Response**: AI can also help predict natural disasters like hurricanes, floods, and wildfires. Early warnings generated by AI can help save lives and protect property.

  - **Example**: AI models are being used by organizations like **The European Space Agency (ESA)** to predict and monitor **wildfires**, using satellite data and machine learning algorithms to identify fire-prone areas and track their progression in real-time.

3. **Waste Management**: AI is helping to optimize **waste management** processes, making recycling and disposal more efficient and environmentally friendly. By analyzing waste patterns and automating sorting processes, AI can increase recycling rates and reduce landfill waste.

   - o **Smart Sorting**: AI-powered robots equipped with **computer vision** can be used to sort recyclable materials such as plastic, glass, and metal from waste streams. These robots can identify and separate items more quickly and accurately than humans.

- **Example**: **AMP Robotics** uses AI-powered robots to automate the sorting of recyclables in materials recovery facilities (MRFs). The robots use computer vision to identify different materials and pick them off the conveyor belt for recycling.
  - **Waste-to-Energy**: AI can also be used in waste-to-energy processes, where waste materials are converted into renewable energy. AI can optimize the conversion process by predicting the best way to extract energy from waste and reduce the environmental impact of waste disposal.
    - **Example**: AI can help optimize **landfill gas-to-energy** systems, where methane gas produced by decomposing organic waste is captured and converted into electricity.

---

### *Example: AI in Smart Grids for Energy Distribution*

One of the most promising applications of AI in the environmental space is in the development of **smart grids** for energy distribution. A smart grid is an intelligent electrical grid that uses AI, sensors, and communication technologies to monitor and manage the flow of electricity in a more efficient and reliable way.

1. **How Smart Grids Work**: Smart grids use real-time data from **sensors** and **smart meters** installed in the grid to monitor energy consumption and adjust energy distribution. AI systems process this data to predict energy demand, identify inefficiencies, and optimize the grid's performance.

    o **Example**: During periods of high demand, AI algorithms can predict when and where the grid will experience stress and make adjustments in real time to ensure a stable power supply. For example, AI can automatically increase energy generation from renewable sources, like solar or wind, during peak hours, or direct power to areas where demand is highest.

2. **AI for Energy Demand Prediction**: One of the key functions of smart grids powered by AI is **energy demand forecasting**. By analyzing historical data, weather forecasts, and consumption patterns, AI can predict when electricity demand will spike and adjust the energy distribution accordingly.

    o **Example**: In **California**, energy companies use AI to predict the demand for electricity based on factors like temperature, time of day, and past usage. This allows them to efficiently allocate energy from both renewable sources and the grid to meet demand without overloading the system.

3. **Integration of Renewable Energy**: AI plays a key role in **renewable energy integration**. It helps manage the fluctuating nature of renewable energy sources, such as wind and solar, which depend on weather conditions. AI can predict energy production from renewable sources and balance it with demand, reducing reliance on fossil fuels and minimizing carbon emissions.

   o **Example**: AI algorithms can forecast wind or solar power generation and adjust grid distribution to ensure the energy is used efficiently. For example, if there's an excess of solar energy during the day, AI can store the surplus energy in batteries or redistribute it to areas with high demand.

4. **Fault Detection and Maintenance**: AI can also be used for **predictive maintenance** in smart grids. By monitoring equipment and analyzing real-time data, AI systems can detect potential failures in the grid and schedule maintenance before breakdowns occur, improving reliability and reducing downtime.

   o **Example**: AI-based systems can predict when equipment like transformers or power lines might fail and alert operators to conduct repairs or maintenance, preventing major power outages and ensuring consistent service.

In this chapter, we explored how **AI is revolutionizing the environment** by providing **sustainable solutions** for energy distribution, climate modeling, and waste management. AI is transforming **smart grids** by optimizing energy distribution, improving the integration of renewable energy sources, and forecasting energy demand. AI is also being applied in areas like **climate prediction**, **waste management**, and **sustainable agriculture**, helping mitigate environmental challenges and improve resource efficiency. As AI continues to advance, it will play an increasingly important role in creating a more sustainable, efficient, and environmentally friendly future.

# CHAPTER 21: THE FUTURE OF AI: TRENDS AND POSSIBILITIES

*Emerging Trends in AI*

Artificial Intelligence is advancing rapidly, and as it continues to evolve, it is poised to transform even more aspects of our daily lives. From breakthrough technologies to new applications across various industries, AI is expanding its reach and capabilities. Below are some of the key **emerging trends** in AI that will shape its future:

1. **AI in Autonomous Systems**: One of the most exciting developments in AI is the creation of increasingly autonomous systems. Autonomous vehicles, drones, and robots are moving from concept to reality, powered by AI technologies like **reinforcement learning** and **computer vision**. These systems will become more capable of performing tasks independently, transforming industries such as transportation, logistics, and defense.

o **Trend**: **Fully autonomous transportation** (self-driving cars, drones, etc.) will continue to grow, moving from being niche technologies to mainstream solutions for mobility and goods delivery.

2. **AI and Ethics**: As AI becomes more embedded in critical systems, ethical considerations will take center stage. Ensuring AI fairness, accountability, and transparency will be crucial for widespread adoption. Researchers and policymakers are increasingly focused on developing ethical frameworks for AI, particularly in areas like **bias**, **privacy**, and **data governance**.

o **Trend**: There will be greater emphasis on **AI governance** and the creation of **ethical guidelines** to ensure AI systems are developed and deployed responsibly, ensuring they align with human values.

3. **AI in Healthcare Innovation**: AI's impact on healthcare will continue to expand, especially in **personalized medicine**, **drug discovery**, and **robot-assisted surgery**. AI-powered systems will help doctors diagnose diseases faster, discover new treatments, and provide tailored care based on genetic and environmental factors.

o **Trend**: **AI-driven precision medicine** will gain traction, offering treatments tailored to individual patients' genetic makeup, health history, and lifestyle.

4. **Natural Language Processing (NLP) Advancements**: NLP, a subfield of AI that allows machines to understand, interpret, and generate human language, is evolving rapidly. As AI becomes better at understanding context, sentiment, and nuance in language, it will improve how we interact with machines.

   o **Trend**: The continued development of more **advanced NLP models**, capable of generating human-like language, will lead to breakthroughs in **chatbots, virtual assistants,** and **automated content creation**.

5. **AI in Creative Industries**: AI is no longer limited to tasks like data analysis or automation. It is now being used to create music, art, and even literature. AI-generated content is becoming more sophisticated, leading to the emergence of **AI-driven creativity tools** that assist human creators.

   o **Trend: Generative AI** will increasingly be used to create art, design, and entertainment content, blurring the lines between human and machine creativity.

6. **AI and Quantum Computing**: The combination of AI with **quantum computing** is another frontier that promises to accelerate AI's capabilities. Quantum computers are

capable of solving certain types of problems exponentially faster than classical computers, which could lead to breakthroughs in AI that were previously unimaginable.

- o **Trend**: **Quantum AI** will enable new possibilities in fields such as **optimization**, **drug discovery**, and **material science**, making AI models significantly more powerful and capable of solving complex problems.

---

### *What's Next for AI Research and Innovation?*

AI research is in a dynamic phase of expansion, and future innovations promise to have a profound impact on technology and society. Here are some key areas that will be the focus of AI research and innovation in the coming years:

1. **Explainable AI (XAI)**: As AI systems become more complex, one of the challenges is understanding how they make decisions. **Explainable AI** aims to make AI models more transparent and interpretable, allowing humans to understand the reasoning behind AI decisions.

   - o **Next Step**: Research into **XAI** will ensure that AI systems can be trusted and held accountable, particularly in critical areas such as **healthcare** and

**finance**, where understanding the rationale behind AI-driven decisions is essential.

2. **AI in Augmented Reality (AR) and Virtual Reality (VR)**: The integration of AI with **AR** and **VR** technologies will revolutionize fields like gaming, education, and training. AI can enhance immersive environments by generating real-time interactive content, personalizing user experiences, and providing more natural interactions in virtual spaces.

   o **Next Step**: The combination of **AI, AR, and VR** will create highly immersive environments for applications ranging from **medical training** and **remote work** to **virtual tourism** and **personalized education**.

3. **AI and Sustainability**: As the world grapples with climate change and environmental degradation, AI will play a pivotal role in **sustainability** efforts. AI-powered solutions can optimize energy use, improve waste management, support renewable energy integration, and help monitor environmental changes.

   o **Next Step**: AI will be integral to achieving **sustainable development goals (SDGs)**, helping to address environmental challenges like **climate change**, **biodiversity loss**, and **resource scarcity**.

4. **Human-AI Collaboration**: The future of AI is likely to involve **collaborative intelligence**, where humans and AI

work together to solve problems. Rather than replacing humans, AI will assist in decision-making, problem-solving, and creativity, enhancing human potential.

- o **Next Step**: **AI-enhanced human creativity** and **collaboration** will redefine industries like **design**, **engineering**, and **research**, where AI can augment human expertise and innovation.

5. **AI in Autonomous Systems**: Research will continue to refine **autonomous systems**, such as self-driving cars, drones, and robots. These systems will become increasingly capable of operating in dynamic, real-world environments, with a focus on safety, reliability, and human interaction.

- o **Next Step**: The continued development of **autonomous robots** and **AI-powered vehicles** will reshape transportation, delivery services, and even space exploration.

---

*Real-World Example: AI in Space Exploration*

AI's potential extends to space exploration, where it is being used to enhance missions, automate tasks, and analyze vast amounts of data collected from space. AI is helping space agencies like **NASA** and private companies like **SpaceX** tackle challenges in space exploration.

1. **Autonomous Spacecraft Navigation**: AI is used to navigate spacecraft autonomously, helping to improve mission efficiency and safety. This is particularly important for missions to distant planets, moons, or asteroids, where human intervention may not be possible.

   o **Example**: NASA's **Autonomous Navigation System** (AutoNav) uses AI to autonomously guide spacecraft, like the **Mars rovers**, ensuring they can make real-time navigation decisions without constant communication with Earth. This helps rovers find the best routes across the Martian surface, avoid obstacles, and conduct scientific experiments.

2. **AI in Satellite Data Processing**: Space agencies collect vast amounts of data from satellites, such as imagery of Earth's surface or planetary bodies. AI-powered algorithms can analyze this data more efficiently than humans, identifying patterns and making predictions about weather patterns, climate change, or resource distribution.

   o **Example**: AI is used in **Earth observation satellites** to analyze environmental changes, monitor deforestation, track wildfires, and detect natural disasters, enabling faster responses to climate-related events.

3. **AI for Space Robotics**: AI-powered robots are used in space missions to perform tasks such as repairing satellites, assembling spacecraft, or conducting experiments on distant planets. These robots can make autonomous decisions, reducing the need for human astronauts in dangerous or remote locations.

   o **Example**: The **Rover AI** on Mars is capable of performing complex tasks, such as analyzing soil samples, taking photographs, and even identifying geological features, helping scientists understand the planet without having to physically be there.

4. **AI for Astrobiology**: AI is also being used to search for signs of life beyond Earth. By analyzing data from space probes, telescopes, and even soil samples from other planets, AI algorithms can identify potential biosignatures or signs of microbial life.

   o **Example**: AI models are being developed to process data from Mars and other planets, analyzing the chemistry and geology of soil samples to help determine whether life ever existed in those environments.

In this chapter, we explored the **future of AI**, focusing on **emerging trends** such as **autonomous systems, AI and ethics, AI in healthcare**, **natural language processing**, and **AI in space**

**exploration**. AI is evolving rapidly, and its future research directions will push the boundaries of what's possible, from enhancing human creativity and collaboration to developing fully autonomous systems. Real-world examples, such as AI in **space exploration**, demonstrate how AI is already enabling incredible advancements in fields like **space navigation**, **satellite data processing**, and **astrobiology**. As AI continues to evolve, its applications will likely shape nearly every aspect of society and technology, offering new possibilities and challenges in the years to come.

# CHAPTER 22: AI IN EDUCATION: TRANSFORMING LEARNING

## Introduction: The Changing Landscape of Education

- **Brief Overview**: The traditional education system has remained largely unchanged for centuries, but with the rise of artificial intelligence (AI), a new era of learning is unfolding. AI is reshaping how students learn, how teachers teach, and how educational institutions manage their operations.

- **Current Challenges in Education**: Discuss the challenges facing education today, such as overcrowded classrooms, limited resources, one-size-fits-all teaching methods, and the need for personalized learning. AI has the potential to address these challenges in profound ways.

- **Importance of AI in Education**: Explain the growing role of AI in education, especially how it helps educators cater to the needs of individual students while automating administrative tasks. AI-powered systems have the potential to improve both teaching and learning outcomes by personalizing education and offering real-time feedback.

---

## 1. AI-Powered Learning Platforms: Personalizing Education

- **What is Personalized Learning?**
    - **Definition**: Personalized learning refers to adapting education to meet the individual needs, skills, and interests of students. AI allows for more customized education experiences that can address different learning paces and styles.
    - **AI in Adaptive Learning Systems**: AI-driven learning platforms, such as **Khan Academy** and **DreamBox**, adjust lesson difficulty based on a student's performance, ensuring they receive material suited to their skill level.
- **How AI Adapts to Student Needs**:
    - AI-driven platforms gather data on student interactions and use algorithms to create personalized learning paths. This leads to more efficient learning by allowing students to progress at their own pace, preventing them from falling

behind or becoming bored with material that is too easy.

- o **Example**: **Duolingo** uses AI to personalize language learning based on a user's progress and areas where they struggle. The system adjusts the difficulty of exercises based on past performance and offers challenges to reinforce learning.

- **Benefits of Personalized Learning**:
  - o AI in education helps ensure that no student is left behind. Struggling students receive more support, while high-performing students are consistently challenged. This reduces dropout rates and helps close the achievement gap.
  - o It also allows for more diverse and inclusive education, as AI can cater to different learning styles—whether a student learns best through visual aids, hands-on activities, or written explanations.

---

## 2. AI Tutors and Virtual Classrooms: 24/7 Learning Assistance

- **AI Tutors: A New Era of Student Support**:
  - o AI-powered tutors, like **Socratic by Google** and **Jill Watson** at Georgia Tech, are designed to assist

students in answering questions, explaining concepts, and providing feedback on assignments.

o These AI systems use **natural language processing (NLP)** and **machine learning** to simulate human-like tutoring sessions, making them accessible to students outside of regular classroom hours.

- **How AI Tutors Work**:

  o AI tutors understand the student's queries and respond with explanations, problem-solving steps, or even guide them through step-by-step learning processes. These virtual tutors can also assess the student's understanding in real-time and adjust their responses accordingly.

  o For example, **Jill Watson**, an AI assistant developed at Georgia Tech, was able to answer questions from students in an online class with a high level of accuracy, mimicking the behavior of a teaching assistant.

- **Virtual Classrooms and Interactive Learning**:

  o AI enables the creation of **virtual classrooms** where students and instructors can interact through video, chat, and AI-driven tools. Platforms like **Coursera** and **EdTech applications** use AI to deliver educational content and assess student participation.

o  AI also enhances student engagement by making learning more interactive. Tools like **Quizlet** and **Kahoot** use AI to create gamified learning experiences, which increase student motivation and provide instant feedback.

## 3. AI-Driven Assessment: Efficient and Accurate Evaluation

- **Automating Grading and Feedback**:
    - o  Grading assignments and exams, especially in large classrooms, can be time-consuming for teachers. AI automates grading for quizzes, tests, and assignments, allowing for quicker turnaround times and freeing up educators to focus on more meaningful interactions with students.
    - o  **Example**: **Turnitin** uses AI to check for plagiarism and provide immediate feedback to students on the originality of their work. Similarly, **Gradescope** uses AI to grade and provide feedback on assignments in real-time.
- **AI for Formative and Summative Assessment**:
    - o  AI is not limited to grading but extends to providing both **formative** and **summative assessments**. In formative assessment, AI gives real-time feedback

to students, helping them identify areas that need improvement and guiding them through practice exercises.

o  In summative assessment, AI provides insights into a student's overall progress, including mastery of learning objectives. These data-driven insights enable teachers to adapt instruction as needed and ensure that students receive targeted support.

## 4. AI in Educational Administration: Streamlining Operations

- **Administrative Automation**:
  - o  AI can automate many administrative tasks that schools and universities traditionally handle manually. These include **scheduling, admissions,** and **student attendance**.
  - o  **Example: AI chatbots** can be used for answering common questions about registration, course schedules, and exam dates. This reduces the burden on human staff, allowing them to focus on more complex tasks.
- **AI for Data-Driven Decision Making**:
  - o  Educational institutions are increasingly relying on AI to analyze data for decision-making purposes.

By analyzing student performance, behavior, and engagement data, AI systems can provide insights that help schools improve educational outcomes.

o AI can identify patterns in student behavior, predict dropout rates, and suggest interventions to prevent students from falling behind.

- **Predictive Analytics in Student Retention**:
  - o Predictive analytics powered by AI can help institutions identify at-risk students before they fail or drop out. AI analyzes academic records, attendance data, and other relevant factors to predict a student's likelihood of success, enabling targeted interventions.
  - o **Example**: **Early Alert Systems** use AI to identify students who may need additional support, such as tutoring, counseling, or academic advising, based on early warning signs like poor grades or low engagement.

---

## 5. The Impact of AI on Teachers and Educators

- **Supporting Educators, Not Replacing Them**:
  - o AI should be viewed as a tool that supports and enhances the role of teachers, not replaces them. AI

can handle the administrative tasks, grading, and personalized learning, allowing teachers to focus on fostering creativity, critical thinking, and emotional intelligence—skills that AI cannot replicate.

- o Teachers will still play a crucial role in the educational process by interpreting AI-generated data, offering emotional support, and guiding students through complex, real-world problems.

- **AI as a Teaching Assistant**:
  - o AI can serve as an "assistant" to teachers, providing real-time analysis and insights into student performance and offering recommendations for instructional strategies.
  - o **Example**: AI tools like **Edmentum** provide teachers with personalized teaching recommendations based on data from students' learning patterns, helping to target areas where individual students might need additional help.

## 6. Challenges and Concerns of AI in Education

- **Data Privacy and Security**:
  - o The use of AI in education raises concerns about **student data privacy**. AI platforms gather vast

amounts of personal information, including learning behavior, performance metrics, and even biometric data.

- o Institutions must ensure they comply with data privacy regulations like **FERPA** (Family Educational Rights and Privacy Act) in the U.S. to protect student information.

- **Bias in AI**:
  - o AI models can inherit biases from the data they are trained on, which could lead to unfair or discriminatory outcomes in educational settings. For example, an AI system might unfairly favor students from certain backgrounds or disadvantage those from underrepresented groups.
  - o **Example**: If an AI system is trained on historical data that reflects gender or racial biases, the recommendations it generates might unintentionally perpetuate these biases.

- **Teacher and Student Resistance**:
  - o Some teachers and students may resist the integration of AI into the classroom, fearing that it may diminish human interaction, make education feel less personal, or replace the role of educators altogether.

- Addressing these concerns requires clear communication about how AI can complement traditional teaching methods and provide additional support.

---

- **AI's Expanding Role**:
  - AI is already reshaping education, and as the technology evolves, its impact will only grow. From personalized learning experiences to administrative automation, AI has the potential to make education more efficient, accessible, and tailored to individual needs.
- **Preparing for the Future**:
  - To harness the full potential of AI in education, both educators and students must embrace new technologies and adapt to new ways of learning and teaching. Preparing teachers through training programs and ensuring ethical, transparent AI practices will be crucial in the successful integration of AI into education.
- **A New Era of Education**:
  - AI in education represents a shift toward a more personalized, data-driven, and efficient learning ecosystem. It offers immense possibilities for

transforming the learning experience and addressing long-standing challenges in the education system.

# CHAPTER 23: AI AND CYBERSECURITY: SAFEGUARDING THE DIGITAL WORLD

*Introduction: The Growing Importance of Cybersecurity*

In today's hyper-connected world, cybersecurity has become one of the most critical concerns for individuals, businesses, and governments alike. As we increasingly rely on digital infrastructure for communication, commerce, healthcare, and more, the threats to our online security have also grown. Cyberattacks are evolving in sophistication, and traditional methods of defense are often struggling to keep pace with these advanced threats.

This is where **Artificial Intelligence (AI)** comes into play. AI is transforming the cybersecurity landscape by providing advanced tools to detect, prevent, and respond to cyber threats in real time. AI systems can process vast amounts of data, identify patterns, and adapt to new and evolving threats faster than humans or traditional security systems ever could.

In this chapter, we explore how AI is being used to enhance cybersecurity, focusing on its role in **threat detection**, **incident response**, **data protection**, and **predictive analytics**. We will also discuss the challenges and ethical considerations of AI in cybersecurity and highlight real-world examples of AI-powered cybersecurity applications.

---

### 1. AI for Threat Detection and Prevention

One of the primary uses of AI in cybersecurity is **threat detection**. Traditional methods rely on predefined rules or signatures to identify threats, but these systems are often inadequate against newer, unknown threats (zero-day attacks). AI, particularly machine learning (ML), can significantly improve the ability to detect and prevent cyber threats by learning from data and identifying patterns of malicious activity.

- **Anomaly Detection with Machine Learning**:
  - **Machine Learning** (ML) models are trained to recognize normal patterns of behavior within a network or system. Once trained, the system can detect anomalies—deviations from these normal patterns—indicating a potential cyberattack. This enables AI systems to detect attacks that do not match known patterns, such as **advanced persistent threats** (APTs) or **insider threats**.
  - **Example**: An AI system might detect unusual network traffic patterns, such as large data transfers or access from unfamiliar locations, which could indicate a data breach or ransomware attack.
- **Real-Time Threat Detection**:
  - AI systems can continuously monitor network traffic, endpoints, and other digital assets to identify potential vulnerabilities and threats in real-time. Unlike traditional systems, which may rely on periodic scans, AI can provide continuous monitoring, giving organizations a more proactive approach to cybersecurity.
  - **Example**: AI systems like **Darktrace** use unsupervised machine learning to detect and respond to previously unknown threats. By continuously analyzing network traffic, Darktrace

can identify and respond to cyber intrusions as they happen, often before a human would notice.

- **Predictive Analytics for Threat Forecasting**:
  - By analyzing historical data, AI can predict potential attack vectors and the likelihood of future cyber threats. This can help organizations prioritize their defenses and take proactive measures to shore up weaknesses before they are exploited.
  - **Example**: AI models that use predictive analytics can analyze past breach data and global attack trends to forecast potential threats, allowing businesses to strengthen their security posture in advance.

---

## 2. AI in Incident Response: Automated Defense Systems

Once a cyberattack is detected, rapid response is essential to minimize damage and prevent further compromise. AI can help automate and accelerate the incident response process by quickly identifying the nature of the attack, isolating affected systems, and even taking preemptive actions to stop the attack from spreading.

- **Automated Incident Response**:
  - **AI-driven response systems** can automatically detect an attack and begin executing predefined

defensive actions, such as blocking suspicious IP addresses, disconnecting infected machines, or isolating compromised data. This can drastically reduce the response time and lessen the impact of the attack.

o **Example**: **Cylance**, an AI-based cybersecurity company, uses machine learning to predict and prevent cyberattacks before they occur. It can automatically take action in response to potential threats by stopping malicious processes in real-time.

- **AI-Powered Malware Detection**:
  o AI systems can analyze files and processes on a system to detect and prevent malware infections, including those that might bypass traditional signature-based systems. By using **deep learning** models, AI systems can detect patterns associated with malicious software and stop it from executing.
  o **Example**: **Sophos Intercept X** uses AI to identify malicious software, even zero-day threats, by analyzing the behavior of files and processes on a system rather than relying solely on known virus signatures.

- **Incident Tracking and Forensics**:
  o After an attack has been thwarted, AI can assist in **digital forensics** by analyzing attack vectors,

identifying compromised data, and helping security teams understand how the breach occurred. This can help in patching vulnerabilities and fortifying defenses for the future.

o **Example**: **IBM QRadar** is an AI-powered platform that helps security teams track incidents and conduct post-attack analysis. It integrates with other systems to provide a comprehensive view of the attack, which helps teams assess the damage and prevent similar incidents.

---

### 3. AI for Data Protection and Privacy

Data protection is a fundamental aspect of cybersecurity. With the growing volume of data and increasingly sophisticated threats, organizations must use AI to protect sensitive information and maintain privacy.

- **AI in Data Encryption**:
  - o AI can help encrypt sensitive data both in transit and at rest. AI systems can dynamically adapt encryption strategies based on the nature of the data, ensuring that sensitive information is protected without slowing down system performance.

o **Example**: AI-powered encryption systems can automatically detect sensitive data and encrypt it in real-time. This protects data during transactions or when stored in databases, ensuring it remains secure even if the system is breached.

- **AI for Privacy Compliance**:

  o AI can assist in compliance with data privacy regulations like **GDPR** and **CCPA** by identifying and categorizing personal data across an organization's infrastructure. AI systems can monitor data access, ensure proper handling of sensitive information, and flag any potential breaches of privacy policies.

  o **Example**: AI-powered tools like **OneTrust** help businesses automate privacy compliance by identifying and categorizing data, managing consent, and automating the process of responding to data subject requests.

- **Protecting Against Insider Threats**:

  o Insider threats, whether intentional or accidental, pose a significant risk to data security. AI can analyze user behavior and access patterns to identify potential insider threats, flagging any anomalies that may indicate malicious or careless actions by employees.

- o **Example**: **Microsoft's Azure Sentinel** uses AI to monitor user behavior and detect any suspicious activity. If an employee suddenly accesses sensitive data they normally wouldn't, AI systems can flag it as potentially malicious, helping to prevent data breaches.

---

## *4. The Role of AI in Predicting and Preventing Cyberattacks*

AI's ability to process large amounts of data and identify emerging patterns allows it to predict and prevent cyberattacks before they occur. This proactive approach can help organizations stay one step ahead of cybercriminals.

- **Predictive Threat Intelligence**:
    - o AI models can analyze global threat data, including attack patterns, hacker activity, and emerging vulnerabilities, to predict potential future cyberattacks. By using AI to process this data, organizations can better prepare for and defend against threats that are likely to occur.
    - o **Example**: **CrowdStrike** uses AI and machine learning to provide real-time threat intelligence, identifying attack trends and offering early warnings about emerging cybersecurity threats.

- **Adapting to New Threats**:
  - ○ One of the strengths of AI in cybersecurity is its ability to **learn and adapt** over time. As AI systems are exposed to new cyberattack methods, they continuously improve their detection and response capabilities. This makes AI an invaluable tool for protecting against unknown or novel threats.
  - ○ **Example**: **FireEye** uses AI to continuously learn from previous attacks, adapting its threat detection systems to recognize and mitigate new types of attacks, including polymorphic malware that changes its appearance to avoid detection.

---

## 5. Challenges and Ethical Considerations of AI in Cybersecurity

While AI brings many benefits to cybersecurity, its use also raises several challenges and ethical concerns.

- **Bias in AI Systems**:
  - ○ Like any AI system, cybersecurity tools powered by machine learning can inherit biases from the data they are trained on. If biased data is used, AI models may produce false positives or miss certain types of attacks, potentially leaving organizations vulnerable.

- o **Example**: AI systems that are trained primarily on data from large enterprises may not perform well in small or medium-sized businesses, where attack patterns and data are different.

- **AI-Powered Attacks**:
  - o Just as AI can be used to defend against cyberattacks, it can also be used by cybercriminals to launch more sophisticated attacks. For example, AI can be used to automate phishing attacks or create more convincing deepfakes.
  - o **Example**: **Deepfake technology**, powered by AI, is increasingly being used in cyberattacks to impersonate trusted figures and manipulate targets.

- **Privacy Concerns**:
  - o AI systems that monitor network traffic or user behavior may raise privacy concerns. Organizations must ensure that AI tools do not infringe on individuals' privacy rights while still providing robust security measures.
  - o **Example**: AI-powered monitoring systems that track user behavior could potentially violate data privacy regulations if they access personal information without proper safeguards.

### *Conclusion: The Future of AI in Cybersecurity*

AI is playing a transformative role in the cybersecurity industry, enhancing both threat detection and prevention. By leveraging machine learning, predictive analytics, and real-time automation, AI-powered systems are able to detect emerging threats, respond to incidents swiftly, and protect sensitive data more effectively than ever before.

However, with these advancements come challenges and ethical considerations that must be carefully addressed

# CHAPTER 24: AI IN ENTERTAINMENT: SHAPING THE FUTURE OF MEDIA AND CREATIVITY

*Introduction: The Intersection of AI and Creativity*

Artificial intelligence (AI) has been an incredibly transformative force in the entertainment industry. From **music composition** to **video game development, film production,** and **interactive storytelling**, AI is reshaping how content is created, consumed, and delivered. AI's integration into entertainment doesn't just streamline production; it also opens up new realms of possibility for creative expression. By leveraging AI's ability to analyze vast amounts of data, adapt to user preferences, and even generate original content, the entertainment industry is being fundamentally redefined.

This chapter explores the key ways in which AI is shaping the future of media and creativity, focusing on AI's applications in **music, film and television production, video games,** and **personalized content delivery**. We also look at the impact of AI on **creative professionals**, how AI tools can enhance their work, and the ethical challenges this new frontier presents.

---

## *1. AI in Music: Composing the Future*

AI's role in music production has evolved significantly over the past few years, and its use has expanded beyond merely assisting with sound mixing to actively composing music, creating personalized playlists, and enhancing the creative process.

- **AI-Powered Music Composition**:
  - o AI systems like **OpenAI's MuseNet** and **Aiva** (Artificial Intelligence Virtual Artist) are capable of composing full-length musical pieces in various genres, from classical symphonies to modern pop music. These systems learn from vast datasets of musical compositions, enabling them to generate original pieces that reflect the nuances of specific styles.
  - o **Example**: **Aiva** has been used to compose original classical music that has been performed by real orchestras. Aiva analyzes patterns in classical compositions, understands their structure, and applies this knowledge to create new, original works.

- **AI-Assisted Music Production**:
  - o AI tools like **Amper Music** and **Endlesss** allow musicians to create, remix, and refine tracks with minimal input. These platforms use machine learning algorithms to generate musical ideas based on a user's preferences or the sound they are aiming to create.
  - o AI can also automate tasks in the music production process, such as mixing, mastering, and sound design. For example, AI can balance audio levels

and apply effects like reverb or compression in ways that would traditionally take an engineer hours to fine-tune.

- **Personalized Music Recommendations**:
  - Streaming services like **Spotify** and **Apple Music** use AI to analyze listeners' habits and suggest new music that fits their tastes. By studying user behavior, AI algorithms can create highly personalized playlists and recommend artists or tracks that align with the listener's preferences, helping users discover new music and enriching their listening experience.
  - **Example**: Spotify's **Discover Weekly** playlist is an example of an AI-driven feature that tailors music recommendations to the specific tastes and listening patterns of each user.

---

## 2. *AI in Film and Television Production: Revolutionizing Filmmaking*

The integration of AI in film and TV production is reshaping the entertainment landscape, enabling faster and more cost-efficient productions, while also pushing creative boundaries.

- **AI in Scriptwriting and Storytelling**:

- o AI tools like **OpenAI's GPT-3** are being used to assist writers in generating plot ideas, writing scripts, and even creating dialogue. These systems can analyze existing stories and create new ones, drawing from a deep understanding of narrative structures and character development.
- o **Example**: AI-assisted scriptwriting tools can help writers brainstorm ideas, generate plot twists, or flesh out character dialogue. **Sunspring**, a short film written entirely by an AI, demonstrated the potential of AI in scriptwriting.

- **AI in Visual Effects (VFX)**:
  - o AI is making a major impact in visual effects by automating labor-intensive tasks, such as rotoscoping (isolating objects in frames), background removal, and object tracking. AI models can quickly analyze video frames, extract objects, and apply effects, reducing the time and cost typically associated with post-production.
  - o **Example**: **DeepDream** and **StyleGAN** are AI models that can generate unique and stunning visual effects. These models allow filmmakers to create surreal visuals that might not be feasible through traditional VFX methods.
- **AI for Animation and Character Creation**:

- AI can also be used in animation, particularly in the creation of realistic character movements. Through machine learning and motion capture data, AI systems can learn to mimic human movement and expressions, creating lifelike animated characters.
- **Example**: In the movie **The Lion King** (2019), AI was used to create hyper-realistic animations that closely mimic animal behavior. AI-powered tools were used to automate certain aspects of character animation and scene generation.

- **AI in Editing and Post-Production**:
  - AI tools are increasingly used for video editing and post-production tasks, such as automatic scene selection, color correction, and audio mastering. AI algorithms can analyze raw footage, automatically identify the best shots, and even generate rough cuts based on the director's instructions.
  - **Example**: **Adobe Sensei** uses AI to help automate tasks like color correction and facial recognition during post-production, allowing editors to focus on the creative aspects of filmmaking.

---

### 3. AI in Video Games: Enhancing Play and Development

AI has been a cornerstone of video game development for years, particularly in creating intelligent non-playable characters (NPCs) and building dynamic, immersive game worlds. However, recent advancements in AI are pushing the boundaries of interactive entertainment.

- **AI in Game Design and Development**:
  - AI is being used to design dynamic, immersive, and ever-changing game worlds. AI algorithms can generate game levels, plotlines, and even entire open-world environments autonomously, providing a unique experience for each player.
  - **Example**: In **No Man's Sky**, AI was used to procedurally generate planets, environments, and creatures, ensuring that no two players would ever experience the same game world.
- **AI-Driven NPCs and Dynamic Storytelling**:
  - AI is making NPCs (non-playable characters) smarter, enabling them to adapt to player behaviors, respond with more realistic dialogue, and engage in complex decision-making. This results in a more dynamic, responsive gaming experience.
  - **Example**: **The Elder Scrolls V: Skyrim** uses AI to control NPC behaviors, making them more responsive to the player's actions. For example,

NPCs react differently depending on whether they are allies, enemies, or neutral parties.

- **AI for Procedural Content Generation**:
  - o AI is now used to create massive amounts of content within video games. This includes generating **new levels**, **quests**, **enemies**, and even **story arcs** based on player preferences and behavior. It allows game developers to offer endless content without manually designing every single aspect.
  - o **Example**: **Minecraft**, with its procedurally generated worlds, uses AI to create unique terrains, dungeons, and structures that offer players new experiences every time they play.

- **AI in Player Experience and Personalization**:
  - o AI is also used to personalize player experiences by adjusting the difficulty level, providing tailored challenges, and even modifying in-game events based on the player's preferences and past behavior.
  - o **Example**: **AI in adaptive difficulty** adjusts a game's difficulty in real-time based on the player's performance, ensuring a balanced and challenging experience for players of all skill levels.

## *4. AI in Personalized Content Delivery: Revolutionizing Consumer Experiences*

AI is transforming how consumers interact with media. Streaming platforms and content providers are increasingly using AI to personalize content delivery, improving user engagement and satisfaction.

- **AI-Powered Content Recommendations**:
    - o Streaming services like **Netflix**, **Spotify**, and **YouTube** use AI to analyze user behavior and preferences to recommend TV shows, movies, music, and videos tailored to individual tastes. These recommendations are based on the user's viewing history, search behavior, and even ratings or likes.
    - o **Example**: Netflix's recommendation engine uses a combination of collaborative filtering and content-based filtering to suggest new shows based on what users have watched in the past, as well as what similar users are watching.
- **AI in Marketing and Targeting**:
    - o AI is also reshaping the way entertainment is marketed. By analyzing data from social media, search engines, and customer behavior, AI can predict which types of content will resonate most

with specific audiences, enabling more effective and targeted marketing campaigns.

- o **Example**: **Spotify** uses AI to segment users into distinct listener groups, offering personalized ads or playlists based on their musical preferences and engagement patterns.

- **Interactive and Personalized Storytelling**:
  - o AI enables new forms of **interactive storytelling**, where the narrative adapts based on the viewer's choices. This is a particularly exciting area for the future of media, as it combines AI's ability to generate personalized content with human creativity.
  - o **Example**: **Bandersnatch**, an interactive episode from *Black Mirror*, allowed viewers to make decisions that affected the storyline. This type of interactive content will only become more sophisticated as AI algorithms generate diverse and personalized story arcs.

---

## 5. The Ethical Considerations of AI in Entertainment

While AI offers exciting possibilities for entertainment, it also raises important ethical concerns. The widespread use of AI in media creation and distribution demands careful consideration of its implications.

- **Deepfakes and Misinformation**:
  - AI-powered deepfake technology has made it easier than ever to create hyper-realistic but fake videos. This can be used for entertainment purposes but also poses a risk for spreading misinformation and manipulating public perception.
  - **Example**: Deepfakes can be used to create fake celebrity endorsements, fake political speeches, or even impersonate individuals. The entertainment industry must develop ethical guidelines to prevent the misuse of this technology.

- **Job Displacement for Creatives**:
  - As AI takes on more roles in content creation, questions arise about the impact on human creators. Will AI displace artists, writers, musicians, and other creatives? While AI can enhance creativity, it's important to strike a balance to ensure that human creators still play a central role.
  - **Example**: The rise of AI-generated music, art, and writing could lead to concerns about the loss of originality and artistic value, as machines begin to dominate the creative industries.

- **AI Bias in Content Creation**:
  - AI systems trained on biased data can reproduce and amplify existing biases in content creation. This

could result in media that reflects harmful stereotypes or fails to represent certain groups accurately.

- ○ **Example**: AI-powered content recommendation algorithms may reinforce **filter bubbles**, where users are repeatedly exposed to content that aligns with their pre-existing beliefs, limiting diversity and perspective in media consumption.

---

AI is reshaping the entertainment industry, providing new tools for content creation, distribution, and personalization. From AI-generated music and film scripts to personalized recommendations and interactive storytelling, the future of entertainment is being profoundly shaped by artificial intelligence.

As AI continues to evolve, it will unlock even more creative possibilities for filmmakers, musicians, game developers, and consumers. However, as with all technological advancements, the entertainment industry must navigate the ethical challenges that come with AI, ensuring that it is used responsibly, inclusively, and ethically.

Ultimately, AI has the potential to enhance human creativity, rather than replace it, by providing new tools, insights, and opportunities for innovation. The future of entertainment is an exciting blend of human ingenuity and AI-driven possibilities, paving the way for richer, more dynamic media experiences.

# CHAPTER 25: GETTING STARTED WITH AI: TOOLS AND RESOURCES

*Introduction: Navigating the World of AI*

Artificial Intelligence (AI) is one of the most transformative technologies of our time. From improving healthcare to revolutionizing transportation, AI is being used across almost every industry. However, getting started with AI can be overwhelming for beginners, especially with the rapid pace of advancements in the field. The good news is that there are now many accessible resources, tools, and platforms that make it easier than ever to learn AI and start building your own AI projects.

In this chapter, we will explore how beginners can embark on their AI learning journey, the best free tools, courses, and platforms to use, and provide a hands-on example of building a simple machine learning model using Python. By the end of this chapter, you'll be equipped with a roadmap to start learning AI, along with practical examples and resources to guide you.

## 1. How Beginners Can Start Learning AI

Starting with AI doesn't require a background in advanced mathematics or computer science, though it certainly helps. Many

AI concepts can be learned through practical exercises and exposure to the right tools and resources. Here's a step-by-step guide on how beginners can begin their AI journey:

1. **Understand the Basics of AI**:
   - o Before diving into complex algorithms or models, it's essential to understand the fundamental concepts of AI. AI is a broad field encompassing various subfields, including **machine learning (ML)**, **natural language processing (NLP)**, **computer vision**, and **robotics**.
   - o **Key Concepts**:
     - **What is AI?**: AI refers to the simulation of human intelligence processes by machines, particularly computer systems. These processes include learning, reasoning, problem-solving, and understanding language.
     - **Machine Learning**: A subset of AI, machine learning involves teaching machines to learn from data without being explicitly programmed. It's one of the most important areas of AI today.
     - **Deep Learning**: A subset of machine learning that uses neural networks to process data. Deep learning is used in tasks like

image recognition, speech recognition, and natural language processing.

- **Supervised vs. Unsupervised Learning**: In supervised learning, the model is trained on labeled data, while in unsupervised learning, the model identifies patterns in data without labels.

2. **Learn the Fundamentals of Python**:

   o Python is the most popular programming language for AI and machine learning due to its simplicity and the powerful libraries it offers for AI development. If you're new to programming, start with the basics of Python, including understanding variables, loops, functions, and data structures like lists and dictionaries.

   o **Key Python Libraries for AI**:

     - **NumPy**: For numerical computing and working with arrays and matrices.
     - **Pandas**: For data manipulation and analysis.
     - **Matplotlib and Seaborn**: For data visualization.
     - **Scikit-learn**: For implementing machine learning algorithms.
     - **TensorFlow and PyTorch**: For deep learning and neural networks.

3. **Start with Machine Learning**:

   o Machine learning is the most approachable starting point for beginners. Focus on understanding the three main types of machine learning:

     - **Supervised Learning**: Where the model is trained using labeled data (e.g., predicting house prices based on historical data).

     - **Unsupervised Learning**: Where the model identifies patterns and structures in data without labels (e.g., clustering similar data points together).

     - **Reinforcement Learning**: Where the model learns by interacting with an environment and receiving feedback (e.g., AI playing video games).

4. **Hands-On Practice**:

   o The best way to learn AI is by doing. Once you have a basic understanding of machine learning and the necessary programming skills, start experimenting with simple projects. Practice with real-world datasets to build models and gain practical experience.

   o Participate in AI challenges and competitions such as those on **Kaggle**, which offer hands-on experience and allow you to apply your skills to solve real problems.

---

## 2. Free Tools, Courses, and Platforms for Learning AI

Many high-quality AI resources are available for free or at minimal cost, making AI education accessible to anyone with an internet connection. Below are some of the top tools, courses, and platforms you can use to learn AI:

1. **Online AI Courses and Tutorials**: There are numerous free online courses that cover AI and machine learning from the basics to advanced concepts. Some of the best platforms for learning AI are:

   o **Coursera**:
      - **Machine Learning by Andrew Ng**: A must-take course for beginners, this course covers fundamental machine learning concepts, algorithms, and practical applications.
      - **AI For Everyone**: Also by Andrew Ng, this course provides an introduction to AI from a non-technical perspective, focusing on its societal impacts and real-world applications.

   o **edX**:

- **AI for Robotics**: This free course by Georgia Tech introduces AI concepts through robotics. It's a great resource if you're interested in combining AI with robotics.

  o **Fast.ai**:
    - Fast.ai offers **Practical Deep Learning for Coders**, a hands-on, project-driven course that teaches deep learning in a practical and beginner-friendly manner.

  o **Kaggle**:
    - Kaggle offers **free courses** on machine learning, deep learning, and data science. Kaggle is also a great platform for accessing real-world datasets and engaging in competitions that will improve your practical AI skills.
    - Kaggle's **Python** and **Machine Learning** tutorials are designed for beginners and cover foundational concepts with hands-on examples.

2. **AI Learning Platforms**: These platforms offer tools to help you learn and practice machine learning:

   o **Google Colab**:

- Google Colab is a free cloud-based platform that allows you to write and execute Python code in a notebook environment. It's a great place to learn, experiment with machine learning models, and access GPUs for heavy computations, all for free.

  o **Jupyter Notebooks**:

    - Jupyter is an open-source platform used by data scientists for interactive computing. It's perfect for experimenting with machine learning models and visualizing results.

  o **TensorFlow Playground**:

    - TensorFlow Playground is an online tool where you can visualize and experiment with neural networks in your browser. It's great for beginners to understand how deep learning models work.

3. **Books and Reading Resources**: Several books offer in-depth coverage of AI and machine learning concepts:

  o **"Hands-On Machine Learning with Scikit-Learn, Keras, and TensorFlow"** by Aurélien Géron: A highly practical book that covers everything from basic machine learning to deep learning and neural networks using Python.

- o **"Deep Learning with Python"** by François Chollet: Written by the creator of Keras, this book provides an excellent introduction to deep learning using Python and Keras.
- o **"Python Machine Learning"** by Sebastian Raschka: A great resource for understanding how to build machine learning models using Python.

---

## 3. Example: Building a Simple Machine Learning Model with Python

Let's go through a simple example of building a machine learning model using Python. For this example, we will use the **scikit-learn** library, which is one of the most popular libraries for machine learning in Python.

**Goal**: We will build a model that predicts whether a person has diabetes based on a dataset of medical attributes.

1. **Step 1: Install the Necessary Libraries**

    First, we need to install the necessary libraries: scikit-learn, pandas, and matplotlib.

    bash

    pip install scikit-learn pandas matplotlib

2. **Step 2: Import the Libraries**

Now, let's import the libraries we need.

python

```
import pandas as pd
import numpy as np
from sklearn.model_selection import train_test_split
from sklearn.preprocessing import StandardScaler
from sklearn.linear_model import LogisticRegression
from sklearn.metrics import accuracy_score, confusion_matrix
import matplotlib.pyplot as plt
```

3. **Step 3: Load the Dataset**

For this example, we will use the **Pima Indians Diabetes Dataset**. This dataset contains medical attributes such as **blood pressure, glucose levels, BMI**, etc., and we are predicting whether a person has diabetes or not.

python

```
url = "https://raw.githubusercontent.com/jbrownlee/Datasets/master/pima-indians-diabetes.data.csv"
columns = ['Pregnancies', 'Glucose', 'BloodPressure', 'SkinThickness', 'Insulin', 'BMI', 'DiabetesPedigreeFunction', 'Age', 'Outcome']
data = pd.read_csv(url, names=columns)
```

4. **Step 4: Split the Data into Features and Target**

Now, we'll split the data into features (X) and the target variable (y).

python

```
X = data.drop('Outcome', axis=1)
y = data['Outcome']
```

5. **Step 5: Split the Data into Training and Testing Sets**

We will now split the data into training and testing sets using **train_test_split**.

python

```
X_train, X_test, y_train, y_test = train_test_split(X, y, test_size=0.2, random_state=42)
```

6. **Step 6: Data Preprocessing**

Standardizing the data is crucial for machine learning models, especially when features have different scales. We use **StandardScaler** to standardize the data.

python

```
scaler = StandardScaler()
X_train = scaler.fit_transform(X_train)
X_test = scaler.transform(X_test)
```

7. **Step 7: Train the Model**

   We will use **Logistic Regression**, a simple yet effective model for binary classification problems like this one.

   python

   ```python
   model = LogisticRegression()
   model.fit(X_train, y_train)
   ```

8. **Step 8: Make Predictions**

   After training the model, we can use it to make predictions on the test set.

   python

   ```python
   y_pred = model.predict(X_test)
   ```

9. **Step 9: Evaluate the Model**

   We evaluate the model using accuracy and confusion matrix.

   python

   ```python
   accuracy = accuracy_score(y_test, y_pred)
   print(f"Accuracy: {accuracy * 100:.2f}%")

   cm = confusion_matrix(y_test, y_pred)
   print(f"Confusion Matrix:\n{cm}")
   ```

## 10. Step 10: Visualizing the Confusion Matrix

We can use **matplotlib** to plot the confusion matrix for better visualization.

python

```
fig, ax = plt.subplots()
ax.matshow(cm, cmap='coolwarm', alpha=0.7)
for i in range(cm.shape[0]):
    for j in range(cm.shape[1]):
        ax.text(j, i, cm[i, j], ha='center', va='center', color='black')
plt.title('Confusion Matrix')
plt.xlabel('Predicted')
plt.ylabel('Actual')
plt.show()
```

## *4. Next Steps and Further Learning*

After completing your first project, here are some recommended next steps:

- **Explore More Datasets**: Websites like **UCI Machine Learning Repository** and **Kaggle** offer a wealth of datasets for practice.
- **Take More Advanced Courses**: As you grow more comfortable with AI and machine learning, move on to more advanced courses like **deep learning** or **reinforcement learning**.

- **Experiment with Different Models**: Try experimenting with various machine learning models (e.g., decision trees, random forests, SVMs) and comparing their performance.

Starting your AI journey might seem daunting at first, but with the right resources and tools, it's possible to learn and build your own AI models. This chapter has provided a clear path for beginners to follow, offering useful resources, free tools, and practical examples to get started. By taking small steps and gradually building your knowledge, you'll soon be able to apply AI concepts to real-world problems and take part in the exciting future of artificial intelligence.

# CONCLUSION: THE FUTURE OF AI – CHALLENGES, OPPORTUNITIES, AND ETHICAL CONSIDERATIONS

### *1. Recap of AI's Current Impact*

As we've explored in the previous chapters, **Artificial Intelligence (AI)** is no longer just a futuristic concept; it is a dynamic, transformative force reshaping industries, economies, and societies. From **healthcare** and **education** to **entertainment** and **cybersecurity**, AI's footprint is expanding rapidly, offering both remarkable opportunities and significant challenges. In the chapters before, we've seen how AI is enabling **personalized learning**, improving **medical diagnostics**, creating **interactive media**, and even transforming the way we think about **security** and **privacy** in our digital world.

We have discussed how AI is already playing a role in:

- **AI in Healthcare**: Revolutionizing medical diagnostics, drug discovery, and personalized treatments.
- **AI in Education**: Personalizing learning paths and transforming teaching and administrative practices.

- **AI in Cybersecurity**: Defending against increasingly sophisticated cyber threats through intelligent threat detection and automated response.

- **AI in Entertainment**: Transforming how content is created, consumed, and personalized, and driving innovation in film, music, gaming, and interactive media.

- **AI in Environmental Sustainability**: Providing intelligent solutions to address global environmental challenges such as climate change, waste management, and renewable energy.

Each chapter has demonstrated the breadth of AI's impact, and in many ways, we are only scratching the surface of what is possible.

---

## 2. The Transformative Power of AI Across Industries

AI has proven its potential to transform industries in both fundamental and subtle ways. It is helping industries achieve previously unimaginable feats—whether it's **autonomous driving** that may redefine our roads, **smart grids** in energy that optimize power distribution, or **AI-generated art** that challenges our perception of creativity.

In industries like **manufacturing** and **logistics**, AI-powered robots and algorithms are streamlining production, optimizing inventory management, and improving delivery logistics. In **agriculture**, AI is enabling more efficient farming practices, including precision farming that uses data from sensors to monitor crops and reduce waste.

The application of AI in **personalized medicine** and **education** shows how it can make day-to-day life better by providing tailored solutions that are more responsive to individual needs, reducing inefficiencies, and improving outcomes. By analyzing vast datasets, AI systems are helping practitioners make better-informed decisions, whether it's a doctor choosing the best treatment for a patient or a teacher adjusting the curriculum for students based on their learning speeds.

We are witnessing the evolution of AI's role, moving from specialized systems to more integrated, autonomous tools that have the potential to improve productivity across the board. This shift is helping organizations of all sizes and sectors drive innovation, reduce costs, and unlock new value.

---

### 3. AI's Role in Solving Global Challenges

Beyond practical applications, AI has a critical role to play in tackling some of the world's most pressing challenges. From **climate change** to **healthcare disparities**, AI is a tool that offers solutions that are both scalable and adaptable.

- **Environmental Sustainability**: AI can optimize energy use and create more efficient energy grids, improve waste management processes, and provide predictive insights into environmental changes. These applications will be essential in addressing the climate crisis by helping reduce carbon footprints, supporting the transition to renewable energy, and aiding in conservation efforts.

- **Health Equity**: AI is also making healthcare more accessible and equitable by providing diagnostic tools and treatments that can be implemented remotely, bringing high-quality care to underserved areas. By improving diagnostics, predicting patient outcomes, and enabling faster responses, AI is helping save lives and improve quality of life globally.

- **Disaster Management and Crisis Response**: AI systems can predict and monitor natural disasters, enabling faster and more accurate responses. Whether it's early warnings for hurricanes or real-time damage assessments after earthquakes, AI-powered technologies are providing critical support for disaster management.

Through these applications, AI is proving to be not just a tool for convenience but a catalyst for global change. By solving complex, large-scale problems, AI will contribute to creating more sustainable, just, and healthy societies worldwide.

## 4. The Ethical Landscape: Balancing Innovation with Responsibility

With AI's increasing capabilities, it's essential to highlight the ethical challenges it presents. As powerful as AI can be, it must be developed and deployed in ways that benefit all of humanity, without exacerbating inequality or causing harm.

**AI and Bias**: One of the most pressing concerns with AI is the potential for bias in decision-making. AI models learn from data, and if that data is biased, the AI systems will reflect those biases in their predictions and decisions. This has serious implications, particularly in areas like criminal justice, hiring practices, and healthcare, where biased decisions can have life-altering consequences.

**Privacy and Surveillance**: As AI systems collect and analyze more personal data to create more personalized experiences, concerns around privacy intensify. AI tools can monitor everything from online behavior to personal interactions, raising questions about data ownership, consent, and surveillance. It's critical that the development of AI systems respects individuals' privacy and complies with data protection laws like GDPR and CCPA.

**Accountability in AI Decision Making**: As AI systems become more autonomous, determining responsibility for their actions becomes increasingly complex. Who is to blame if an AI system makes a harmful decision? Is it the developer, the user, or the machine itself? These are questions that need careful thought, particularly in life-critical applications like self-driving cars or autonomous weaponry.

**Ethical AI Design**: AI development must be transparent, fair, and designed to align with ethical principles. Encouraging the inclusion of diverse voices in AI design and fostering global collaboration on AI standards can help ensure that AI serves the collective good, rather than concentrating power or perpetuating inequality.

---

## 5. The Future of AI: Opportunities and Risks

As we look to the future of AI, there are immense opportunities as well as significant risks to consider. In the coming decades, AI will likely become even more integrated into our lives, but it is crucial to approach this future with foresight and caution.

**Opportunities for the Future**:

- **Autonomous Systems**: The development of self-driving vehicles, drones, and robots will revolutionize industries such as transportation, logistics, and manufacturing.
- **Improved Healthcare**: AI will continue to drive advancements in personalized medicine, real-time

diagnostics, and drug discovery, leading to longer, healthier lives.

- **Smarter Cities**: AI can be used to manage everything from traffic flow to waste management, helping to make cities more sustainable and livable.

- **Enhanced Creativity**: AI has the potential to augment human creativity in areas like art, music, film, and writing, producing new forms of expression and entertainment that blend human intuition with machine power.

**Risks and Challenges**:

- **Job Displacement**: Automation, driven by AI, will undoubtedly lead to job displacement in many sectors, and the workforce will need reskilling to adapt to new roles.

- **Weaponization of AI**: The development of AI-powered weapons and autonomous drones raises serious ethical concerns about the future of warfare.

- **AI Dependency**: As AI takes on more responsibilities, there's a risk that humans may become overly reliant on technology, leading to a loss of critical thinking skills and judgment.

The future of AI is ultimately shaped by the choices we make today. Through responsible development, regulation, and collaboration, AI can be harnessed for the common good, opening up new possibilities for solving some of the world's most persistent challenges.

---

### 6. The Role of Humans in an AI-Driven World

While AI continues to grow in sophistication, it's important to remember that humans will remain at the center of AI's impact. AI is not a replacement for human intelligence but rather a tool that enhances human capabilities. The synergy between human intuition and AI's data-processing power will be key to solving complex problems and creating value across various industries.

The human element in AI development—creativity, empathy, and ethical judgment—will be irreplaceable. As AI systems take on more autonomous roles, humans will still be needed to guide, oversee, and make the final decisions about their use. AI can support and amplify human capabilities, but the responsibility for the ethical and thoughtful deployment of AI will always rest with people.

### 7. Conclusion: Embracing the Future of AI with Caution and Curiosity

AI is poised to change the world in ways we can only begin to imagine. From transforming industries to solving global challenges, AI holds immense promise. However, with this promise comes the responsibility to ensure AI is developed and used ethically, transparently, and for the benefit of all.

As we move forward, it is important to approach the future of AI with both **curiosity** and **caution**. The key to harnessing the potential of AI lies not just in the technology itself, but in the values we instill in its development and application. By focusing on collaboration, inclusivity, and ethical decision-making, we can shape an AI-powered future that enhances human well-being, drives innovation, and addresses the most pressing challenges of our time.

The next chapter in AI's journey has already begun, and as we continue to explore its potential, we must remember that the future of AI is not just about machines; it is about creating a better, more equitable world for humanity.

This conclusion ties together the main themes of your book and reflects on the vast potential of AI, the responsibilities it brings, and the considerations for its future development. You can expand upon these sections with more real-world examples, case studies, and reflections to reach the desired word count.

www.ingramcontent.com/pod-product-compliance
Lightning Source LLC
LaVergne TN
LVHW051323050326
832903LV00031B/3332